My name _____

My phone # _____

My violin teacher _____

I0622171

Kaleidoscopes

FOR VIOLIN

BOOK 2

a child-centered, Kodály-inspired
approach to violin study

BY ELISE WINTERS

KALEIDOSCOPES

ISBN 978-1-959675-11-2

Book 2 focuses on by-ear learning. Access these recordings and begin listening daily!

Listen on Spotify:

Violin & Piano

discoverviolin.org/book2-violin

Voice (with lyrics)

discoverviolin.org/book2-voice

Also available on Apple Music, YouTube Music, and other major platforms.

Table of Contents

Scales & Technique

Repertoire

Reference

Note on the capitalization of titles: The title for each song is capitalized according to the grammatical conventions of the corresponding language. Thus, the titles of the French, Swedish, and Slovak songs capitalize only the first word. An exception is made when these titles appear within an English sentence or phrase. In this case the English convention is used.

Articles & Supplemental Material

Skills Introduced

in Kaleidoscopes Book 2

Pitch Decoding

Hearing higher, lower, and the same

Singing on pitch

Searching methodically for a given note

Isolating challenge areas

Listening for mismatches

Left-Hand Skills

Rotation of the left arm

Shifting within a piece

Lowered 1st finger

Vibrato

Differential use of the 4th finger

Bowing & Rhythm

Beautiful tone on full bows

Memorized bowings

Slurs

Mixed articulations within one song

Bow lifts on pickup notes

"Long" staccato

Anchored lift

Spiccato

Varying bow speeds on one bow

Crescendo within a single bow

Crescendo over several notes

Dotted rhythms

Grace notes

Accents

"Swung" rhythm

Uneven bow division

♩♪ rhythm in 6/8

Rapid 16th notes (Schradieck)

Meter

Pickup notes

Playing with the metronome

Distinguishing duple & triple meter

Three beats per measure

Mixed meter

Ties

Music Theory

Organization of beat & rhythm

First and second ending

Absolute note names

Major and relative minor

Chromatic scale

Order of Sharps

Keys & Scales

Two-octave scales

Two keys within one song

Transposition into relative minor

E minor

Tonicization to the dominant

Bb Major / G minor

C Major / A minor

Expressive & musical skills

Stage presence during piano interludes

Expressive playing

Ritard

Phrasing

Dynamic changes

Listening to (and matching) the piano part

Other skills

Daily review of songs

Weekly musical exploration (by composer/artist)

Following the music notation while listening

Segmenting piece into more difficult sections

Pronunciation of titles in French, German & Swedish

Sharing decision-making during the practice

Scales &
Technique

D Major Two-Octave

Preparation for pieces that have both 1st to 3rd position within songs (Spreading Chestnut, Lavender's Blue, etc.)

Two Scale Patterns

Use these scale patterns on this and other scales to increase your speed and agility in a new key or hand position.

Notice that there is a pattern on each scale note, including on *ti* — and that the *ti* pattern actually goes higher than *do*!

In many scales, this *ti* pattern may need to be modified as desired to stay within the current hand frame. One good option is offered below.

Rising Triples

Broken Thirds

TEACHER NOTE

All scales are learned with independent octaves, to help make conscious the location of tonic in each key. The scales may be through-played upon graduating the book.

The order of scales is a suggestion, and can be modified by the teacher as needed. It tracks the order that the keys appear in the Book 2 repertoire, with a few bonus scales added for the purpose of comprehensiveness.

Rhythm & Bowing Patterns Part I

Use these patterns to workshop your bow technique and deepen your mastery on all of the Book 2 keys.

Peanut Brittle   Peanut Butter Cracker   Raisin Bread

Gooseberry Pie   Gooseberry, Gooseberry   Bread & Cheese

Waffles for Breakfast   Gingersnap, Gingersnap   Kiwi

Huckleberry, Huckleberry   Strawberry, Blueberry Ice Cream

Pivoting the Left Arm

The role of the left arm is to "carry" the fingers to each string, rather than the fingers reaching across. We might call this the "elbow train."

Practice the elbow pivot: 1) silently, without fingering; 2) silently, tapping the first finger; 3) with the bow. Notice that the violin and bow arm rotate in parallel.

The first finger should contact the string on the tip of the finger or thumb-side corner. *This exercise builds upon the "Finger Magnets" and "Sleeping Unicorn" from Book 1.*

G Major Two-Octave

This is the first two-octave scale introduced. Note that there are TWO finger patterns, one for each octave.

Once this is mastered, practice the different levels of the left arm.

Scale Cycle: B♭ Major / G Minor

Glädjens Blomster (as G minor). The hand should shifts back one half-step for this scale.

B♭ Major Two-Octave

This is second two-octave scale introduced in Book 2.

Rhythm & Bowing Patterns Part II

The patterns above are notated in G Major, but can be played in any key (e.g. in the key of the relevant song).
A whole note (or similar) may be substituted for the last pattern of each octave, to provide a musically satisfying ending.

Scale Cycle: C Major / A Minor

Golden Slumbers and Branle (C Major); Glädjens Blomster (for A minor).

For the fourth finger extension (*x4*), keep the third finger anchored, and allow the first finger to release from the string.

Be sure to "scoot" or slide the fourth finger for the extension (it should not "hop" or lift off the string).

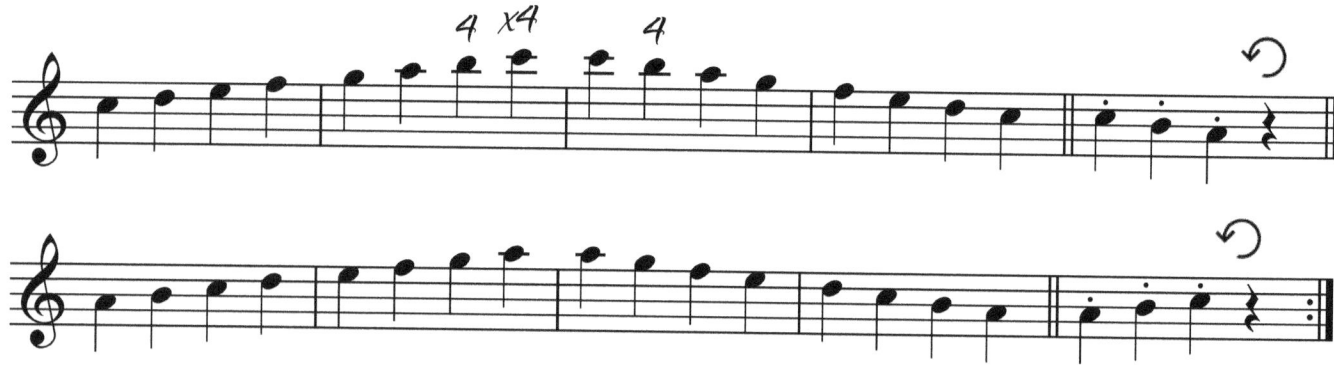

Second Position (F Major)

Preparation for playing the vibrato exercises, which are done in second position.

C Major Two-Octave

This is last of the three two-octave scales introduced in Book 2.

Ringing Notes

The practice partner should rhythmically tap the open string corresponding to the note being played. If the note is in tune, you will hear a beautiful bell sound when the string is tapped. Tapping near the nut makes the best chime sound. Where repeats are marked, play each note 2–4 times.

Choose one set of finger chimes to practice each week.

Third Position, 1ˢᵗ Finger

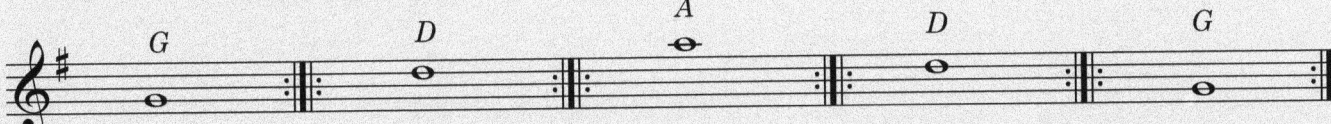

First Position, 3ʳᵈ Finger

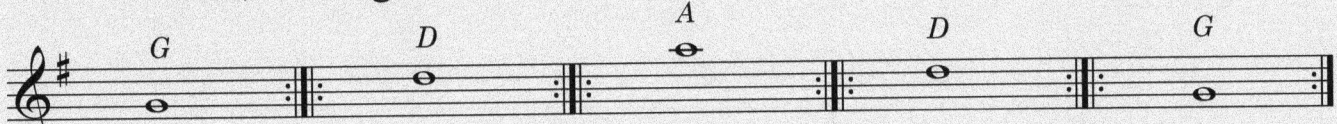

Third Position, 2ⁿᵈ Finger

Test the tunnel: Hold down 2nd finger on the A string, while the practice partner plucks the E string.

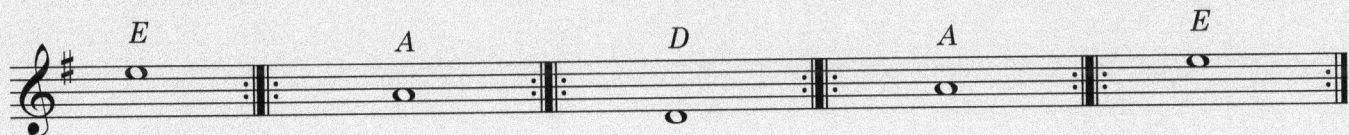

Third Position Ringing Notes

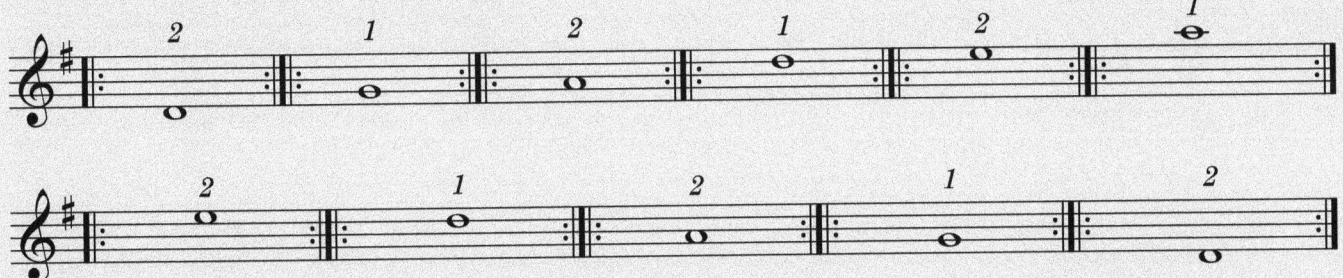

Second Position Ringing Notes

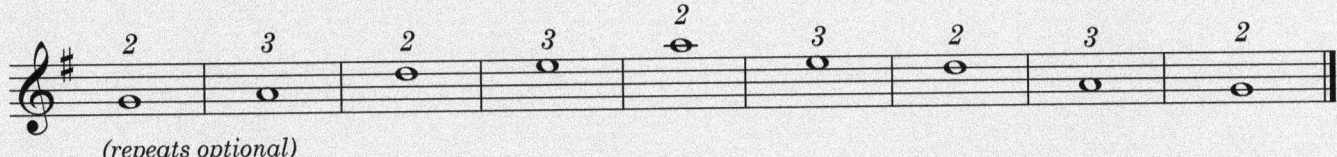

(repeats optional)

Schradieck Etude

Play all lines with 4-note slurs. You can pause between groups initially, closing the gaps when you are ready. The optional "ghost notes" on lines 1–3 can help you to tune your starting note. *All notes are played on the A string.*

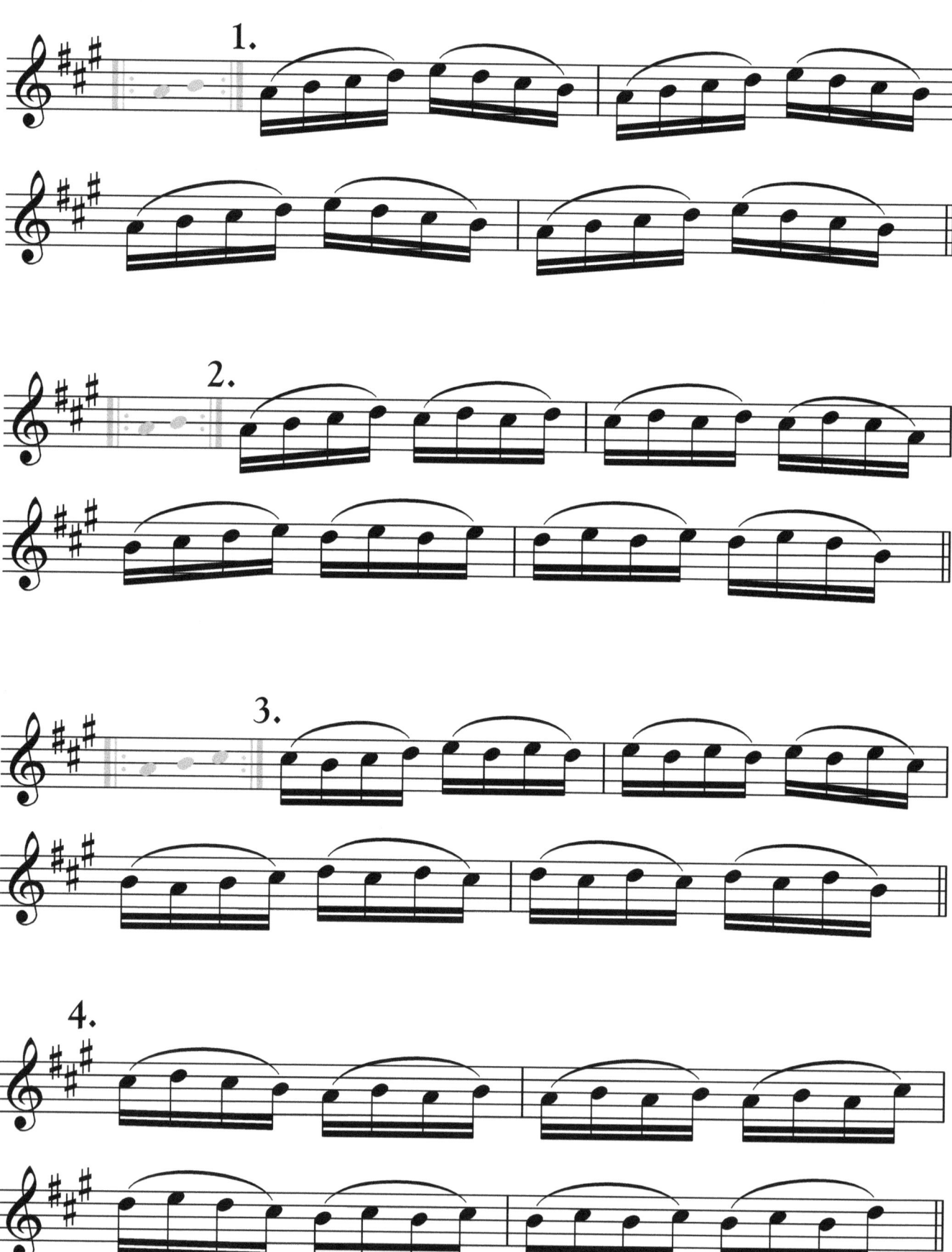

TEMPO
BENCHMARKS

♪ = 70 Reading tempo: 1 note per bow

♪ = 44 Beginner: 2 notes/bow

♪ = 60 Advanced beginner: 4 notes/bow

♪ = 80 Early intermediate: 4 notes/bow

♪ = 110 Intermediate: 4 notes/bow

♩ = 60 Peak intermediate: 8 notes/bow

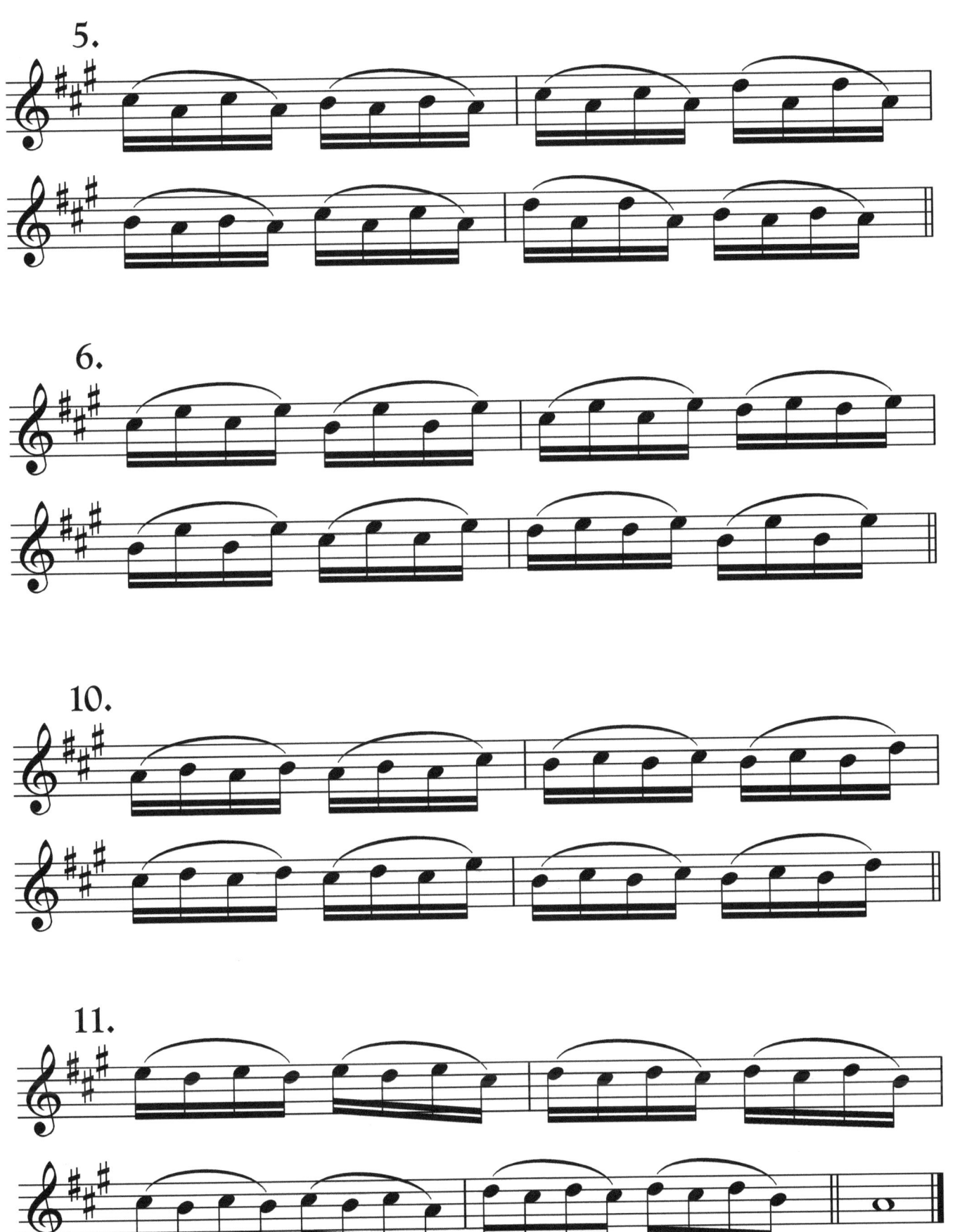

Alphabetic Note Names on the Violin | The D Chromatic Scale

Diatonic means "the notes that are in the current key." *Chromatic notes* are the remaining half-step notes which are not native to the key, but may be added by the composer or player to create different colors in the sound.

In order to name all of the available notes, we use *sharps* and *flats*. A flat (♭) lowers a given white-key note by a half-step. A sharp (♯) raises it by a half-step. Your teacher can show you on a piano how each black key has both a sharp and a flat name.

The notes of the *D chromatic scale* in first position are shown in white below. Notes outside of this one-octave range are shown in gray.

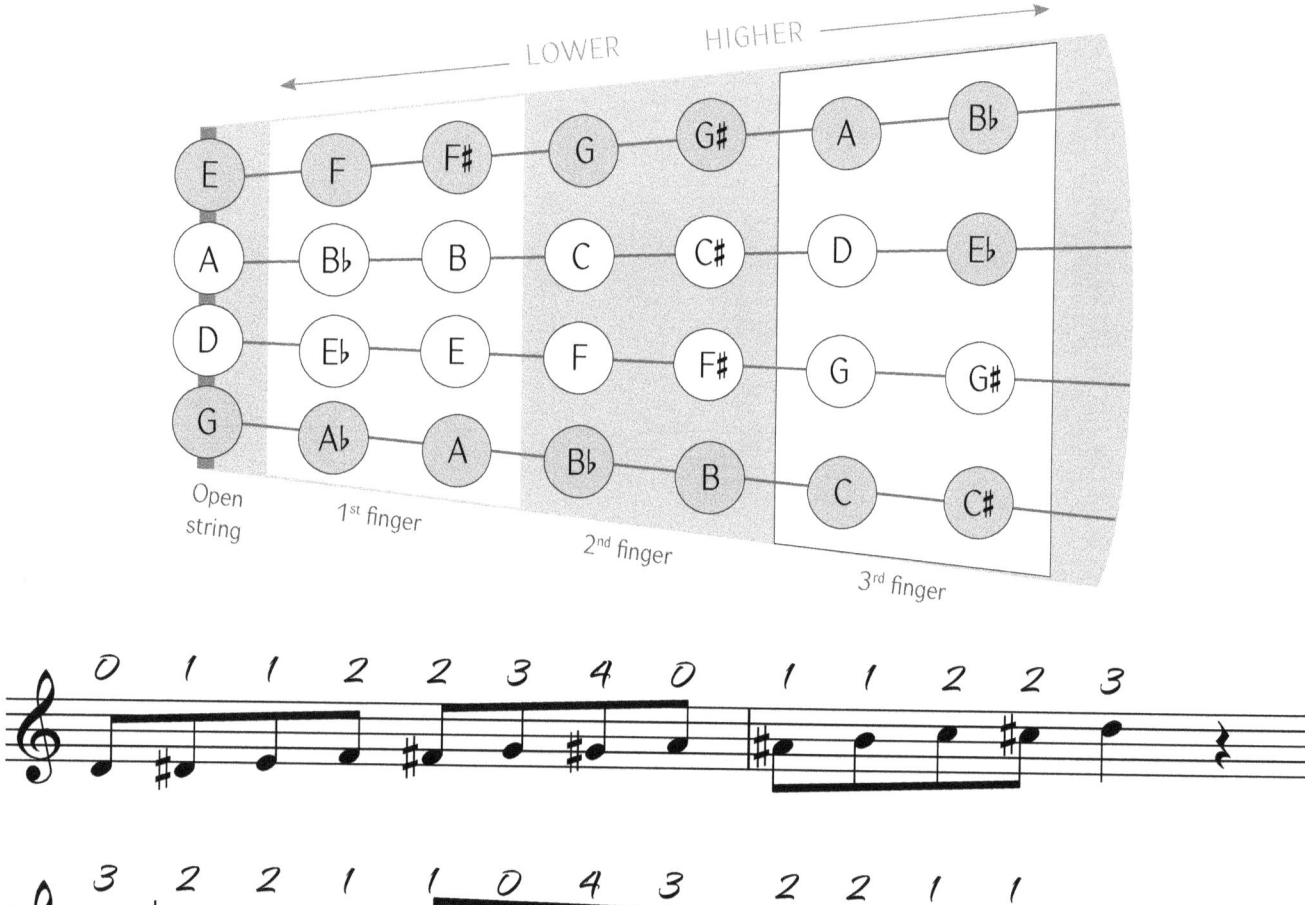

Three things to notice ...

- In printed music, sharps and flats are written *in front of* the note to which they pertain. However, when referring to the note, they are written (and spoken) *after* the alphabetic name (e.g. E♭ or "E flat").

- The ♮ sign means "natural." It is used in music to negate, or neutralize, a previous sharp or flat. So, for example, the E♮ (in the first measure) is simply E.

- Notice that while the 1ˢᵗ measure indicates G♯ and the 3ʳᵈ measure indicates A♭, these are the same note.

Repertoire

Learning Songs by Ear: Where to Start?

Being able to learn songs by ear is the most important skill a musician can have. You will be learning how to do this using the songs in Book 2.

You will notice that some measures of music are left empty to encourage you in this process.

The MOST HELPFUL tool in learning songs by ear is to listen to the recording many, many times a day. Most times when someone is having a hard time learning by ear, it is because they just don't remember the songs. If you listen and sing along A LOT, playing by ear will be much easier!

So, here are the steps to learning the songs by ear:

1. Listen to the song on the recording until you can sing the whole song from memory, with no mistakes or fudging.

    Make sure your singing is as in tune as possible as you're singing along. Practice with the vocal recording until you can match the notes well. This will help you to find the notes more accurately on the violin.

    Find the vocal and violin recordings using the QR codes printed on page iv.

2. Find the starting note of the song on the lyrics page or by looking at the music. (Don't peek at the rest of the notes.)

    Starting with this note, begin working out the rest of the song. This is the "treasure hunt" phase! Keep hunting until you find the right notes. Here are few tips:

    *   Focus on one line at a time.

    *   If you get stuck, simply go back to the beginning.

    *   It also helps to sing the song again, perhaps with the recording.

    *   If you're still stuck, pause for a few days. Take these days to do lots of listening and singing along with the recording. This will help a lot!

    In general, if you're having difficulty with a lot of the songs, it probably means you're not doing enough listening. Listen to the recording at least twice a day.

3. Once you think you can play the whole song by ear, use the printed music to check and see if you got everything right.

4. When you're ready, write in the missing notes. Ask your teacher if you got it right!

For your first by-ear song ... start with whichever one is stuck in your head. This means you're ready to figure it out!

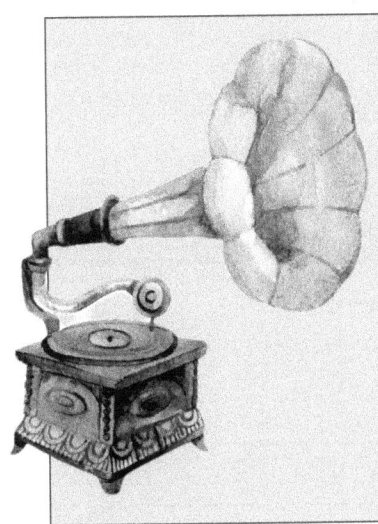

How Should I Listen to the Recording?

There are TWO recordings for Kaleidoscopes Book 2. Volume I is the violin recording. Volume II is vocal (with lyrics). Find both recordings on Spotify, Apple Music, or your favorite platform.

Listen to the entire recording (either volume) TWICE every day for at least TWO MONTHS – during dinner, or while doing homework, doing a hobby, or winding down for the evening. After that, work with your teacher to help create your next listening plan.

Under the Spreading Chestnut Tree

English

D Major

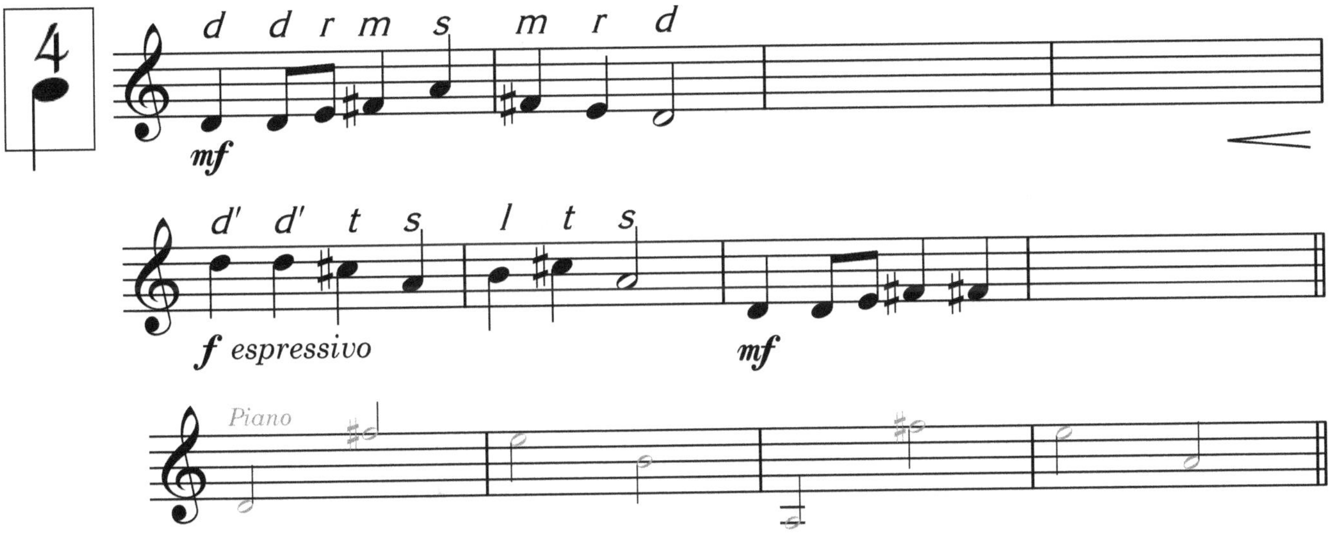

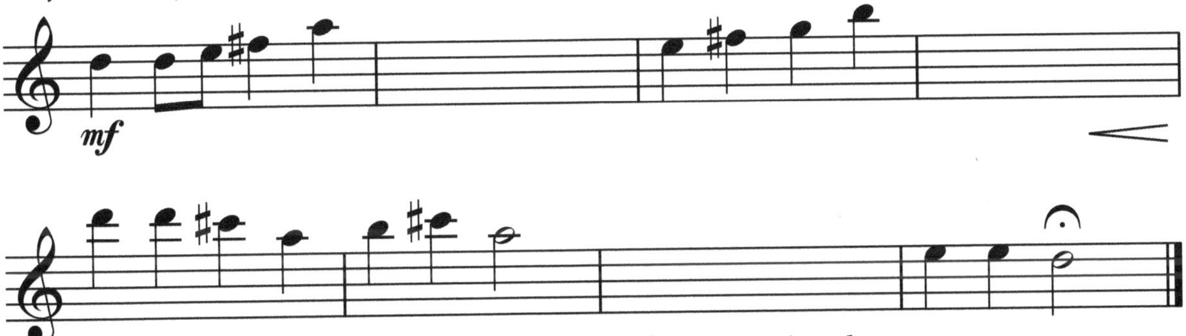

Played in third position (learn by ear)

Under the spreading chestnut tree
When I held you on my knee
We were happy as could be,
Under the spreading chestnut tree.

Hollahi, Hollaho

German

See bowing pattern p.11

Horch, was kommt von draussen rein / Hollahi, hollaho!
Wird wohl mein fein's Liebchen sein / Holla Hia ho!

Hark who beckons at the door / Hollahi, hollaho!
It must be my darling lord / Holla hia ho!

Hark, who beckons at my pane / Hollahi, hollaho!
It must be my darling maid / Holla hia ho!

English translation by Elise Winters © 2017

Can You Find the Hidden Details?

Once you learn the songs by ear, that is just the first step. There are more details to discover!

1. Learn the song by ear. Get it fluent and make sure the notes sound right to you.

2. Open the book and look at the music. What slurs, staccatos, or other markings do you see? Play with the printed music and do your best to add these details.

3. Watch the video of the song on the Kaleidoscopes YouTube channel. The video can also help you to refine these details and add other nuances.

4. Show the song to your teacher at your next lesson, so you can make sure all the notes are correct, and to receive additional guidance.

5. Write in the missing notes! Ask your teacher to make sure they are correct.

6. When you are ready, play along with the video. Be sure to slow it down to the tempo that you can play accurately.

7. Once you have mastered these details to your teacher's satisfaction, you have graduated the first learning.

Later, when you are ready to prepare the piece for recital:

- Listen to the recording, but this time focusing on the piano instead of the violin part. Can you sing bits and pieces of the piano melody?

- Practice with a metronome to help you prepare.

- Now try playing along with the piano solo part. Practice until you can stay lined up.

- Once you can perform the entire song with the piano solo, you have reached full mastery.

Les petites marionnettes

Lay peh-TEET mah-ryo-NETT
French, "The Little Puppets"

Mothers in France typically sing this song to entertain a baby. The "puppets" are her hands and fingers. She acts out each motion of the song — for example, turning the wrists back and forth, hiding her hands behind her, putting them on her head, etc.

A Major

Fine

Da Capo al Fine

Ainsi font, font, font
Les petites marionnettes
Ainsi font, font, font
Trois petits tours et puis s'en vont.

Les mains aux côtés,
Sautez, sautez marionnettes,
Les mains aux côtés
Marionnettes recommencez.

See them turn, turn, turn,
Round and round the little puppets,
See them turn, turn, turn,
Say hello and now they're gone.

Bring them back again,
No more hiding, little puppets,
We shall make amends,
Let the puppets come and play.

English translation by Elise Winters © 2017

Essential Violin Supplies

Now that you are becoming more advanced, you will need a sturdy, full-height Manhasset-style music stand with a solid desk.

You will also need a full-length mirror in your practice room and a dedicated metronome-tuner.

This is also the right time to purchase a wall-mounted violin holder. Spontaneous practicing happens more naturally when the violin is already out of the case!

Les Petites Marionnettes: Piano Countermelody

We often focus so much on the melody, we forget to listen to what's underneath! Familiarize yourself with the piano part in the following ways:

1. **Learn to follow the score.** Each measure of Les Petites Marionnettes has two beats. You can locate them by learning to see notes in groups. *When notes are grouped together, it means they're part of the same beat.* Practice tapping through the whole song, two beats per measure, *without* the music playing.

2. **Coordinate with the recording.** Now tap across the beats again, this time while the recording is playing. Can you end at the same time as the recording? *Tracking the beats is an easy way to follow the score, even if the notes are moving very quickly.*

3. **Find the puppets!** Now do the same thing while truly *listening* to the piano. Try to match the notes you're looking at with what you're hearing the pianist play. Can you hear the puppets in the piano part?

Kookaburra

See bowing pattern p.11

D & G Major

Australian

d'   l   t   d'   l   s

Played in 3rd position

Kookaburra sits in the old gum tree,
Merry, merry king of the bush is he
Laugh, Kookaburra! Laugh, Kookaburra!
Gay your life must be.

Kookaburra sits in the old gum tree
Eating all the gum drops he can see
Stop, Kookaburra! Stop, Kookaburra!
Leave some there for me.

TEACHER NOTE

Helping Students to Decode Songs

Playing the song while the student "grabs" whatever notes they can is a natural, enjoyable, and effective way to assist them in learning songs by ear. A few tips:

- Make sure that they are not watching your fingers. They want to learn how to play by ear, not become a British spy!

- Choose a moderate speed — a bit slower than at-tempo, but fast enough to feel "real."

- Keep your tempo even if the student isn't getting all the notes. Preserving the continuity trains them to stay on their toes and not obsess over a single note. Any notes they can't locate in time, they can figure out the next time around!

- Focus on a whole phrase at a time, rather than small segments. This helps them to think of each phrase as a whole, and avoids any temptation you may have to spoon-feed them. They will get it after a few times through!

- After a few times through, help them reflect on helpful details such as:

  - What is the highest note (in solfège)? (The highest note is often high do.)
  - What is the lowest note (in solfège)? (The lowest note is often low so.)
  - How would you compare mm. 1–2 and mm. 3–4? (Observe patterns and differences.)

- Don't have them write the notes in their music quite yet! They need to practice figuring it out by ear at home, reinforcing what they already discovered in lesson. The repetition is necessary to build their ear and their confidence, making it easier for them to decode the next song.

How Much Should I Practice?

You may discover you are ready to commit to a more significant amount of practice upon entering Book 2. Or it may be that your current amount of practice is still perfect for you. Either way is okay ... so trust yourself!

A committed student who has good attention can consider moving toward ONE HOUR of daily practice. This is long enough to provide solid progress, while short enough to be doable by many students. This hour may be done in one sitting, or divided into 2–3 shorter sessions.

The practice outline below is offered as a starting point. The exact allocation of tasks during the practice will vary day by day and throughout the book.

During your first month in Book 2, talk with your teacher about the length and balance of your practice. Continue checking in and updating your plan every few months.

The most important consideration is that the practice be enjoyable. Doing quality work with love is more important than how much time you spend in the practice room, because long-term enjoyment is the surest path to success.

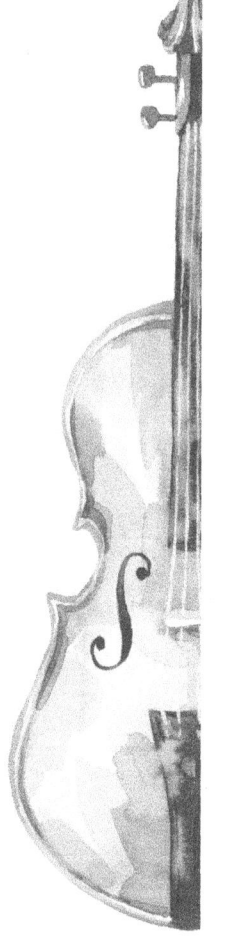

Example Practice Session (1 hour)	
The practice priority can be adjusted by day, with various activities given more time on some days and less on other days.	
Artist listening (a few times per week): 5–10 minutes	
5 minutes	Various scales, with Book 1 and 2 bowing patterns.
5 minutes	Review 4–5 songs which have been graduated recently. Play each one once or as desired.
10 minutes	New Technique | Transposition | Vibrato
10 minutes	Schradieck (or) Lines & Spaces
20 minutes	Learn a new song by ear. Begin mastering it. Add slurs, articulations, and other details to songs which are in the "polishing" stage.
10 minutes	FUN CLOSING Play favorite songs | Musical exploration

TOTAL = 60 minutes

Lavender's Blue

English, circa 1685

D & G Major

Played in third position (learn by ear)

Lavender's blue, dilly, dilly, Lavender's green,
When I am king, dilly, dilly, you will be queen.
Who told me so, dilly, dilly, who told me so?
'Twas my own heart, dilly, dilly, that told me so.

Lavender's green, dilly, dilly, Lavender's blue,
If you love me, dilly, dilly, I will love you.
Let the birds sing, dilly, dilly, And the lambs play;
We shall be safe, dilly, dilly, out of harm's way.

Can You Find the Tricky Part?

Professional violinists break up their music into little pieces, or segments. Otherwise they would spend hours playing through page after page of easy material and the hard parts would never get the attention they need!

It takes mental discipline to break the habit of starting at the beginning and playing through the whole song. However, repeating a single segment takes away the distractions and allows you to give the hard spot your full attention.

Find the part of Lavender's Blue that's harder than the rest. Put a box around this segment.

How many times harder is it than the rest of the song? Five times harder? Ten times? Write this number next to your box. This is how many times to practice this section every day.

Keep getting the tricky spot better. Place a star next to the segment once it is mastered!

Who Are Your Favorite Composers / Artists?

As you become more advanced, you are ready to begin exploring music through focused listening of various pieces and artists. This listening will be valuable as you move to the next level of advancement.

The "Artist Listening" experience is a short interval of focused listening which is done several times each week at the beginning of the practice session. You and your parent will choose a piece to listen to following a chosen theme. Each theme may last a week, month, or longer.

Here are some genre-based themes to explore (notice that instruments besides violin are included):

Violin concertos • String quartets • Baroque / Classical / Romantic composers • Piano concertos • Beethoven symphonies • Impressionist composers • Russian composers • French composers • Cello concertos • Jazz violin • Rock and metal violin • Hip hop violin

You will also enjoy discovering artists and bands with whom you particularly connect. Below are a few to get started:

Classical : Hilary Hahn • Itzakh Perlman • Joshua Bell • Julia Fischer • Midori • Janine Jansen • Nicola Benedetti • Maxim Vengerov • Gil Shaham • María Dueñas • Augustin Hadelich • Lisa Batiashvili

Classical Crossover: Nigel Kennedy • Kronos Quartet • David Garrett • Vanessa-Mae • Esther Abrami

World: L. Subramaniam • Hanine El Alam • Layth Al-Rubaye • Ara Malikian • Alicia Svigals

Fiddle: Michael Cleveland • Alasdair Fraser • Natalie MacMaster • Celtic Woman • Brittany Haas

Pop & Jazz: Black Violin • Brooklyn Rider • Stéphane Grappelli • Quatuor Ebene • Aaron Meyer • Mahavishnu Orchestra • Lindsey Stirling

As you explore, read more about your favorites. How did polio change Itzakh Perlman's life? How was Mozart's relationship with his dad? How did Lindsey Stirling learn to dance and play at the same time?

WRITE DOWN each piece you study in your Weekly Listening log on p.67.

Discovering and listening to music will deepen your appreciation, expand your knowledge, and help you to find your own voice and style!

Periods of Classical Music

The list of eras and composers below represents just a fraction of the world of classical music.

Medieval (c.1150–1400)	Gregorian Chant, Machaut, Hildegard von Bingen
Renaissance (c.1400–1600)	Dowland, Byrd, Palestrina, Tallis
Baroque (c.1600–1750)	Telemann, J.S. Bach, Monteverdi, Corelli, Vivaldi, Handel
Classical (c.1750–1830)	Gluck, Boccherini, C.P.E. Bach, Haydn, Mozart
Early Romantic (c.1830–1860)	Schubert, Beethoven, Smetana, Chopin, Mendelssohn, Schumann, Berlioz, Liszt, Verdi
Late Romantic (c.1860–1920)	Brahms, Dvořák, Holst, Rachmaninoff, Saint-Saëns, Tchaikovsky, Alfven
Impressionist (c.1890–1918)	Ravel, Debussy, Satie, Poulenc, Respighi
Modernist (c.1900–1964)	Copland, Gershwin, Orff, Prokofiev, Shostakovich, Stravinsky

Piper's Tune

English

A piper played a tune, each morning night and noon,
And everyone was happy and gay the live-long day.

Lavender's Blue: Rhythm & Beat

1. In a seated position, establish a steady beat with the left hand. Tap palm-down for beat one, and palm-up for beat two.

2. The right hand will perform the rhythm, and will always be palm-down. Learn the rhythms shown in the warm-up below. Speak the rhythms using the syllables given while tapping it on your lap. *Practice each rhythm until it feels easy before moving on to the next.*

    *   Quarter notes ("TA")
    *   Eighth notes ("ta-di")
    *   Half notes ("TA-AH")

3. Now tap the beat and rhythm of Lavender's Blue, shown below. Speak the rhythm using rhythm syllables as above. Practice until it is easy, accurate, and fast!

Row, Row, Row Your Boat

American

Played in 3rd position

Row, row, row your boat, gently down the stream,
Merrily, merrily, merrily, merrily, life is but a dream.

Beat Discovery of Row, Row Your Boat

Once the student has learned the song, they will need to feel the micro-beat to ensure accurate rhythm. This new micro-beat — triple meter — will be taught using guided discovery. *The steps below may be taught over 1–3 lessons.*

1. Together with the student, sing the song while keeping the beat by marching the feet. If they are marching too fast, encourage the student to lift their legs higher.

2. Now sing the song again, but time tapping the micro-beat using the fingertips in the center of the palm.

3. Now sing the song on a neutral syllable (e.g. "loo") keeping the beat in the feet AND the micro-beat in the palm.

4. Ask the student: How many micro-beats are inside each beat? *If needed, sing the song again, then perform beat and micro-beat alone (without singing) for clarity.*

5. How many beat divisions have we had in previous songs?

6. Once the question has been explored and answered, "sing-tap" the song with the student following the

instructions below. The student should *not* look at the musical notation during this step.

   Sing-tap: Sing on a neutral syllable ("loo") while tapping the index, middle, and ring finger in sequence, following the micro-beat: "1, 2, 3, 1, 2, 3."

7. Now "sing-count" the first two measures with the student. Use a pencil to tap each note on the page while singing the corresponding count. *Eighth notes will receive one tap, dotted quarter notes will receive three, and so on.*

   Sing-count: Point at the notes on the page while singing the micro-beat, "1, 2, 3, 4, 5, 6."

8. "Sing-count" measures 3–4, 5–6 and finally 7–8. Practice each pair of measures until it is mastered and understood.

9. Sing-tap the whole song.

10. Sing-count the whole song again while keeping the macro-beat using a "clap-tap-tap" pattern.

Bluebells of Scotland

Scottish

D major

s d'

t s l fi

ritard.

Oh where, tell me where, has my Highland laddie gone?
Oh where, tell me where, has my Highland laddie gone?
He's gone wi' streaming banners where noble deeds are done,
And it's oh, in my heart I wish him safe at home.

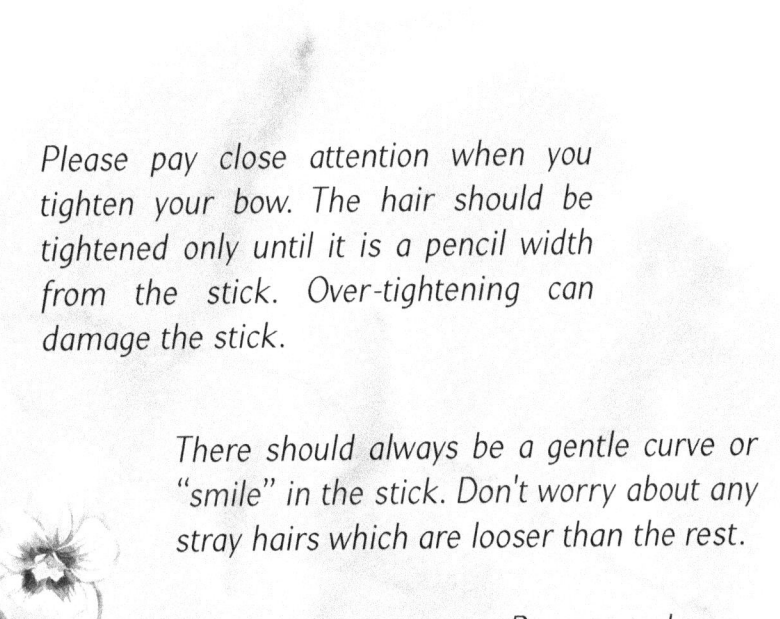

Please pay close attention when you tighten your bow. The hair should be tightened only until it is a pencil width from the stick. Over-tightening can damage the stick.

There should always be a gentle curve or "smile" in the stick. Don't worry about any stray hairs which are looser than the rest.

Be sure to loosen your bow at the end of every practice.

Polly Wolly Doodle

American

Oh, I went down south for to see my Sal,
singing Polly Wolly Doodle all the day,
My Sal she is a spunky gal,
sing Polly Wolly Doodle all the day.

I came to a river and couldn't get across
Sing Polly wolly doodle all the day
I jumped on a gator and thought he was a hoss
Sing Polly wolly doodle all the day.

Refrain
Fare thee well, fare the well,
fare thee well my fairy fay; for I'm
Goin' to Lou'siana for to see my Susy-anna
singing Polly Wolly Doodle all the day.

The melody of "Polly Wolly Doodle" can be found in the 1979 romantic comedy Baton Baton Mein (बातों बातों में).
Composed by Rajesh Roshan, one of the songs in the movie uses the melody of the first two lines of "Polly Wolly
Doodle." The rhythm is slightly different to match the Hindi words, but the melody is unmistakable.

Petit oiseau

Peh-TEET wah-ZOH
French, "Little Bird"

ritard

Entendez-vous sur l'ormeau,
Chanter le petit oiseau?
Tra la la-la-la-la la-la-la-la la,
L'oiseau, sur l'ormeau.

Softly from the forest still,
Do you hear the whippoorwill?
Tra la la-la-la-la la-la-la-la la,
Forest still, whippoorwill.

Har du sett min far

Swedish, "Have You Seen My Father"

Har du Sett is a bouncing game. The word " tocka" is archaic.

‖: Har du sett min far, tocken häst han har,
Tocka lår, tocka ben, tocka skutt han tar, :‖

See the chestnut mare, she's lady fair,
See her trot with my pa through the market square.
But the dapple mare, she's extraordinaire,
She can leap through the air like a snowshoe hare.

English translation by Elise Winters © 2017

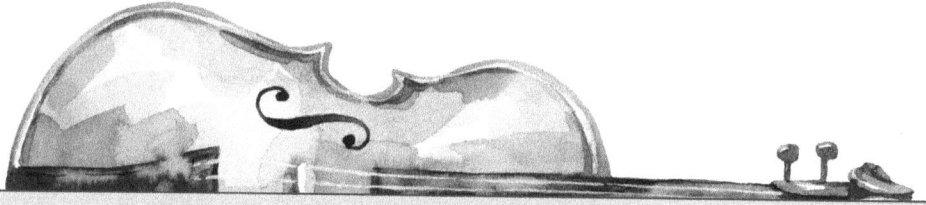

Violin Repair Do's and Don'ts

There are three repairs that it is fine for parents and old-enough students to do at home:

- **Replacing your violin strings**. Strings become "false" over time, and should be changed at least once a year. You'll want to begin doing this yourself either now or in the near future. Always take off just one string at a time (if you take them all off, your bridge will fall over). Tutorials can be found online.

- **Straightening the bridge**. Check your bridge each time you tune your violin; it should always sit perpendicular to the violin top. If it begins leaning over as a result of being bumped, it can become permanently warped. *A leaning bridge should be fixed immediately*. Good video tutorials are available online.

- **Tighten a loose chinrest**. This is an easy fix. Just insert a thick paperclip into the hole on the barrel and rotate clockwise to tighten it. Wittner brand chinrests require a eyeglasses screwdriver to tighten.

The following repairs must be performed by a luthier, and should never be tried at home:

- **The ivory has fallen off the tip of the bow, the metal ferrule has detached, or any other bow repair**. Each part of the bow must remain individually adjustable for the bow to function, and should never be glued. ALL bow repairs should be done by a luthier.

- **The fingerboard has detached from the neck, the wood has broken, or a seam has opened**. Luthiers use specialized glue for violin repairs. Household glues like wood glue or superglue will cause permanent damage to your instrument.

- **There is a scratch or dent in the varnish**. There are various types of varnish, so any varnish repair must be matched to your individual instrument.

- **The soundpost has fallen over**. This is a quick and easy fix, but requires a specialized tool which your local shop will have.

Trying to do the above repairs yourself may save the cost of the repair, but will irreparably damage the violin in the process.

Being handy is great for replacing a board on the back deck, but please trust your luthier to get your violin back in good working order!

Giroflé, girofla

Jee-roh-FLAY, jee-roh-FLAH
French
"Giroflé is a woman's name; "girofla" is a nonsense word.

so fi   *s t d*

‖: Que t'as de bel-les fil-les, Giroflé, girofla!
Que t'as de bel-les fil-les, L'amour m'y comp-t'ra. :‖

‖: So pretty, fair and charming, girofla, Giroflé,
Allow me, sir, to court your daughter if I may. :‖

VOCABULARY
**First &
Second Ending**

Sometimes a repeat has a different ending the second time.

The "first ending" is played the first time, but skipped the second time. The "second ending" is played instead.

Find the endings shown below in *Giroflé, Girofla* above.

Play the first ending, then repeat back to the nearest ‖: ("begin repeat") sign.

Then, on the second play-through, skip the first ending and use the second ending instead.

Practice Concept

(use this for all songs)

Find the hardest part of your songs and play this part
8–12 times each day until it is mastered.

Play the part you've chosen.

Make sure your brain is "on" and
you're thinking about your goal.

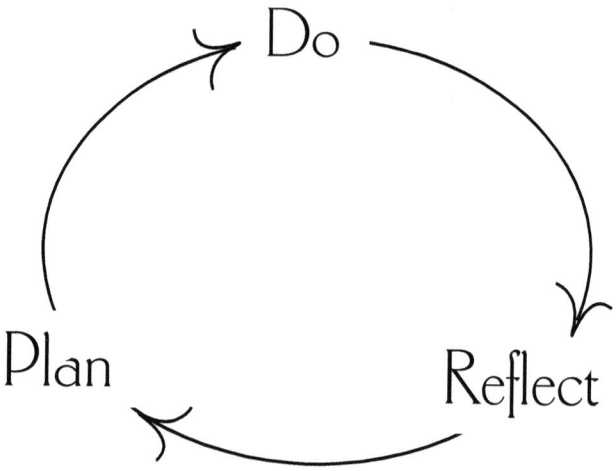

Do

Plan

Reflect

Choose what to focus on.

This should be the ONE thing that is
most important to you.

(You can pick the same thing several
times in a row, until you're happy with
how it went.)

Think about how it went.

What could be better?

Think about how you can fix
whatever didn't work well.

Nu ska vi skörda linet idag

Nu SKAH vee SHOR-dah LIN-et ee-DAHG
Swedish, "We Harvest the Linen Today"

See bowing pattern p.5

A Major

♩ = 88–138

Nu ska vi skörda linet idag,	Come harvest linen, come to the field,
Häckla det väl och spinna det bra.	Come, comb it through and spin on the wheel,
Sen ska vi sömma skjorta och kjol,	Come wind the bobbin, weave on the loom,
Svänga oss glatt i dansen.	Feet dancing on the treadle.
Dunk, dunk, dunk, dunk, dunk, dunk:	Dum, dum, dum, dum, dum, dum,
Vävstolen slår, spolen den går.	Thread on the loom, cloth fill the room,
Dunk, dunk, dunk, dunk, dunk, dunk,	Dum, dum, dum, dum, dum, dum,
Svänga oss glatt i dansen.	Feet dancing on the treadle.

English translation by Elise Winters © 2017

TEACHER NOTE

Skörda Linet Bow Division Exercise

There are two distinct approaches possible for the bow division in Skörda Linet: 1) The bow speed remains consistent, and the bow travels among tip, middle, and lower half; or 2) The player varies the bow speed slightly in order to stay in the middle region of the bow. The latter approach requires greater flexibility and control.

All students will benefit from practicing traveling among bow regions — both those students for whom this is the ideal skill level, as well as those who are ready to try the second approach.

Nu ska vi skörda linet idag (piano)

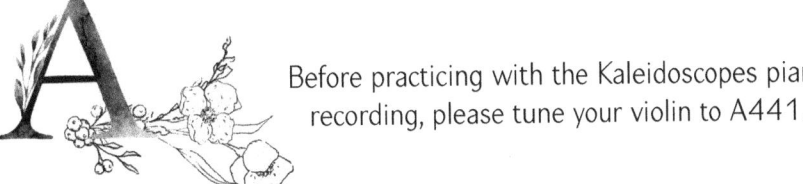

Before practicing with the Kaleidoscopes piano
recording, please tune your violin to A441.

What Can the Matter Be

English

Oh, dear! What can the matter be?
Oh, dear! What can the matter be?
Oh, dear! What can the matter be?
Johnny's so long at the fair.

He promised to buy me a trinket to please me
And then for a smile, oh he vowed he would tease me
He promised to buy me a bunch of red roses
To tie up my bonnie brown hair.

E Minor Transposition

Learning the minor scale | Preparation for Dobrú Noc

G Major	e minor		G Major	e minor	
		Scale			Row, Row
		All My Little Ducklings			Button You May Wander
		Mary Had a Little Lamb			Kookaburra
		Twinkle, Twinkle			Lavender's Blue
		Frere Jacques			Petit oiseau

Ein Männlein Steht im Walde

Īne MENN-line shteht im VAL-duh

German, "A Little Man Stands in the Forest"

See bowing
pattern p.5

Ein Männlein steht im Walde ganz still und stumm.
Es hat von lauter Pu_rpur ein Mäntlein um.
Sagt, wer mag das Männlein sein,
Das da steht im Wald allein
Mit dem purpu_ rroten Mäntelein?

Who is that little fellow with the cloak of red,
In forest quiet, a black top hat upon his head?
Pardon, sir, why do you stay?
Why do not you haste away?
With your satin black hat and cape of red?

SPOKEN:
Who is this little man I see
Who waits alone near yonder tree,
It must the rose-hip berry be.

What is this song about? (Hint: It is not about a man with a red cloak.) _____

With this in mind, how would you describe the personality of the narrator? _____

Dobrú noc

DO-broo NOTES
Slovak, "Good Night"

e minor

Dobrú noc, má milá, dobrú noc,
nech je ti sám Pán Boh na pomoc.
‖: Dobrú noc, dobre spi,
nech sa ti snívajú sladké sny. :‖

Stars in the sky and the moon above,
Close your eyes and sleep, my love.
‖: Angels nigh, God on high,
Dream sweet dreams till morning light. :‖

English translation by Elise Winters © 2017

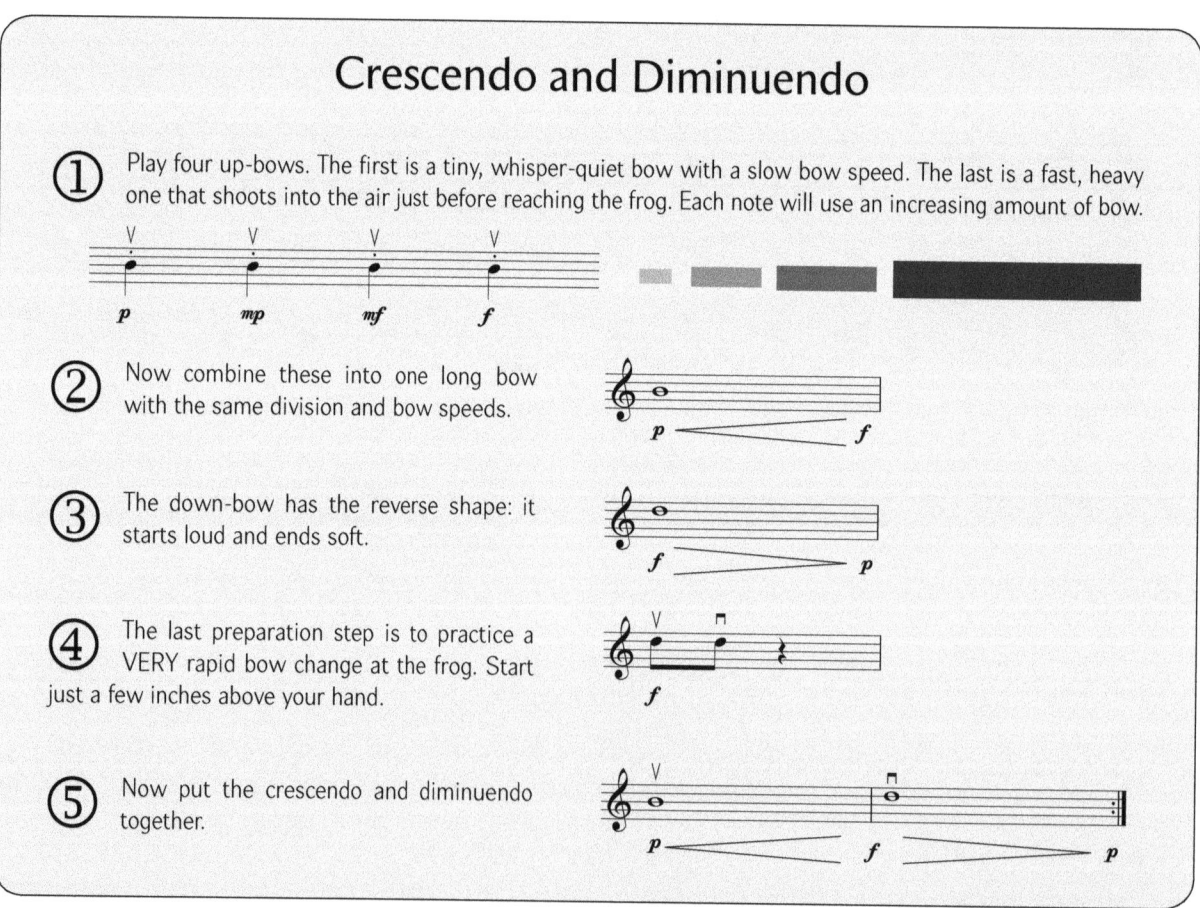

Crescendo and Diminuendo

① Play four up-bows. The first is a tiny, whisper-quiet bow with a slow bow speed. The last is a fast, heavy one that shoots into the air just before reaching the frog. Each note will use an increasing amount of bow.

② Now combine these into one long bow with the same division and bow speeds.

③ The down-bow has the reverse shape: it starts loud and ends soft.

④ The last preparation step is to practice a VERY rapid bow change at the frog. Start just a few inches above your hand.

⑤ Now put the crescendo and diminuendo together.

Galway Piper

Irish

Every person in the nation / Or* of great or humble station
Holds in highest estimation / Piping Tim of Galway.
Loudly he can play, or low** / He can move you fast or slow
Touch your hearts or stir your toe / Piping Tim of Galway.

When he walks the highway pealing / Round the head the birds come wheeling
Tim has carols worth the stealing / Piping Tim of Galway
Thrush and linnet, finch and lark / To each other twitter "Hark!"
Soon they sing from light to dark / Pipings learnt in Galway.

* *"Or" in this context means "whether."*
** *"Low" in this context means "softly"*

Diagonal 3rd finger
workout

TEACHER NOTE

This song is notated with a key signature for D Major even though the song is in A Major. This is not an error, but rather is intended to highlight the presence of G♯ (as low *ti* — the *ti* below *do*).

In each song in Kaleidoscopes Book 2, the key of the song is given above the song. Before practicing the song, the student should play the relevant scale. The student is not yet expected to understand how the key signature relates to the key; this concept will be formally introduced later in the book.

紅葉 (Momiji)

MOH-mee-jee
Japanese, "Autumn Leaves"

Akino yuuhini teru yama momiji
Koimo usuimo kazu aru nakani
Matsuwo irodoru kaedeya tsutawa
Yamano fumotono susomoyo.

Tanino nagareni chiri uku momiji
Namini yurarete hanarete yotte
Akaya kiirono iro samazamani
Mizuno uenimo oru nishiki.

Autumn leaves of maple / Gold and crimson, garnet glow
Mossy green the stream flows / Cloud on the mountain, breezes blow.
Satori-no-mado / Autumn passing, winter snow,
Crimson leaves are falling / Winter comes once more.

English translation by Elise Winters © 2017

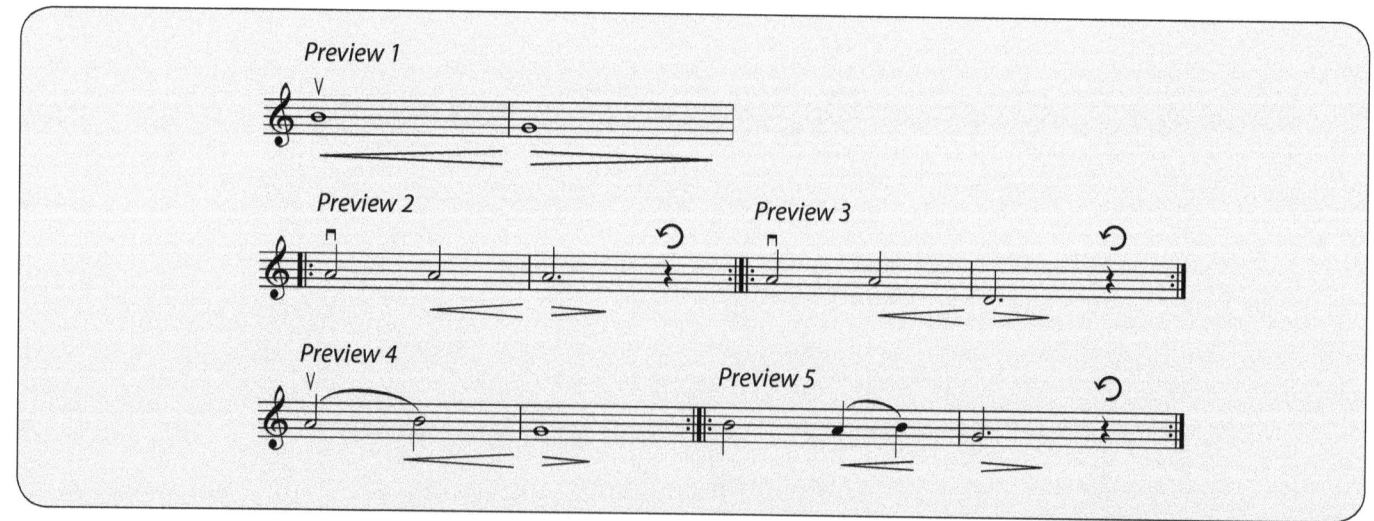

Rising of the Moon

This song is an Irish ballad recounting a battle with the
British Army during the Irish Rebellion of 1798.

John Keegan Casey
circa 1798

e minor

Oh! then tell me, Shawn O'Ferrall, / Tell me why you hurry so?"
"Hush, *ma bouchal*, hush and listen" / And his cheeks were all a-glow.
"I bear orders from the captain, / Get you ready quick and soon,
For the pikes must be together / At the risin' of the moon."

Out from many'a mudwall cabin / Eyes were watchin' through the night.
Many'a manly breast was throbbin' / For the blessed warnin' light.
Murmurs passed along the valley / Like the banshee's lonely croon,
And a thousand blades were flashin' / At the risin' of the moon.

Well they fought for poor old Ireland / And full bitter was their fate
Oh! what glorious pride and sorrow / Fill the name of Ninety-Eight.
Yet, thank God, e'en still are beatin' / Hearts in manhood's burning noon,
Who would follow in their footsteps / At the risin' of the moon!

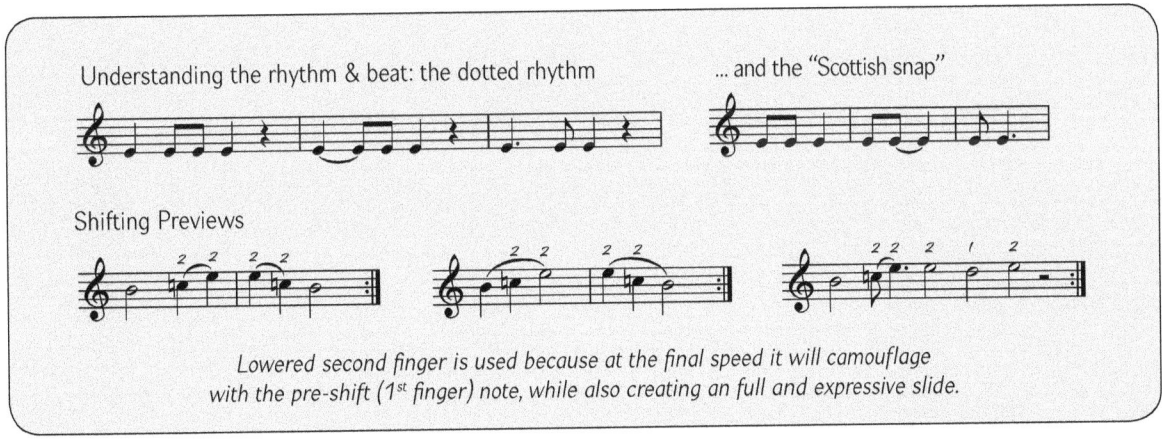

Lowered second finger is used because at the final speed it will camouflage
with the pre-shift (1ˢᵗ finger) note, while also creating an full and expressive slide.

Introduction to Spiccato

Descending rainbows
Create down-bow and up-bow rainbow shapes in the air, above the string.

Gradually lower these shapes to the string, until each rainbow collides with the string at the bottom. Let the bow bounce off the bottom.

Spiccato with string crossing

The trampoline motion of spiccato uses all of the bouncy, springy elements of our violin equipment: the strings, bow hair, and bow stick.

The bow will move in an arc shape, or upside-down rainbow. Most of the stroke is "off the string," with a brief collision at the bottom of each stroke.

The fingers should be medium firm in order to create a good bounce, while flexible enough to cushion the impact.

To reduce the impact noise ("scratch" sound), tilt the bow stick slightly toward the fingerboard. The right hand and right arm will correspondingly rotate slightly up and over. Tilting the bow allows you to "slice" rather than "smack" the string, which reduces noise and instability.

As a side benefit, when you tilt the stick it will now be resting slightly on the fingertips, reducing the load on the pinky.

As you get more proficient, increase the richness of your sound by sloping the sides on your arc — in other words, changing from a bowl shape to a saucer.

Always focus on the elliptical shape, not the landing; and make sure not to use your eyes (this will make it harder to sense the balance and motion of your arm).

Spiccato is fairly easy as long as the bowhold is correct and well-balanced. Even small bowhold imbalances will be magnified by spiccato; the bowhold will become rigid and you will constantly feel like you're about to lose your grip on the stick.

If the bowhold needs work or the pinky is not strong enough to maintain its curve, delay the spiccato learning for a month or two and focus on further developing the bowhold and strengthening the pinky.

For more tips on refining and shaping your spiccato, read "Dimensions of Spiccato" on page 49.

Pont d'Avignon

POH dah-veen-YOH
French, "Bridge to Avignon"

Instructions on p.40

When the lyrics of the song say *comme ça* ("this way"), it is a cue for the dancers improvise whatever movements they wish. The singer can enjoy making up different characters in each verse for the dancers to improvise: for example, musicians, carpenters, elephants, etc.

Refrain
Sur le pont d'Avignon
L'on y danse, l'on y danse
Sur le pont d'Avignon
L'on y danse tout en rond.

Les beaux messieurs font comme ça
Et puis encore comme ça.
[Refrain]

Les belles dammes font comme ça
Et puis encore comme ça.
[Refrain]

Refrain
B'neath the bridge of Avignon
There is dancing, there is dancing,
B'neath the bridge of Avignon
There is dancing all around.

The handsome boys dance this way,
Then they do it that way.
[Refrain]

The pretty girls dance this way,
Then they do it that way.
[Refrain]

Similarly to Galway Piper, the key signature is notated in A Major (even though the song is in E) in order to highlight the presence of D♯.

Shortnin' Bread

American

Mama's little baby loves shortnin', shortnin',
Mama's little baby loves shortnin' bread.
Mama's little baby loves shortnin', shortnin',
Mama's little baby loves shortnin' bread.

Three little children a'layin in bed,
Two were sick and the other 'most dead.
Sent for the doctor, the doctor said,
"Feed those children on shortnin' bread."

[Refrain]

Green Grow the Lilacs

American

G Major

x1 means lowered (extended) first finger.

Green grow the lilacs all sparkling with dew.
I'm lonely, my darling, since parting with you,
But by our next meeting I hope to prove true,
And change the green lilacs to the red white and blue.

I wrote my love letters in rosy red lines,
She sent me an answer all twisted in twines,
Saying, "Keep your love letters and don't waste your time,
Just you write to your love and I'll write to mine."

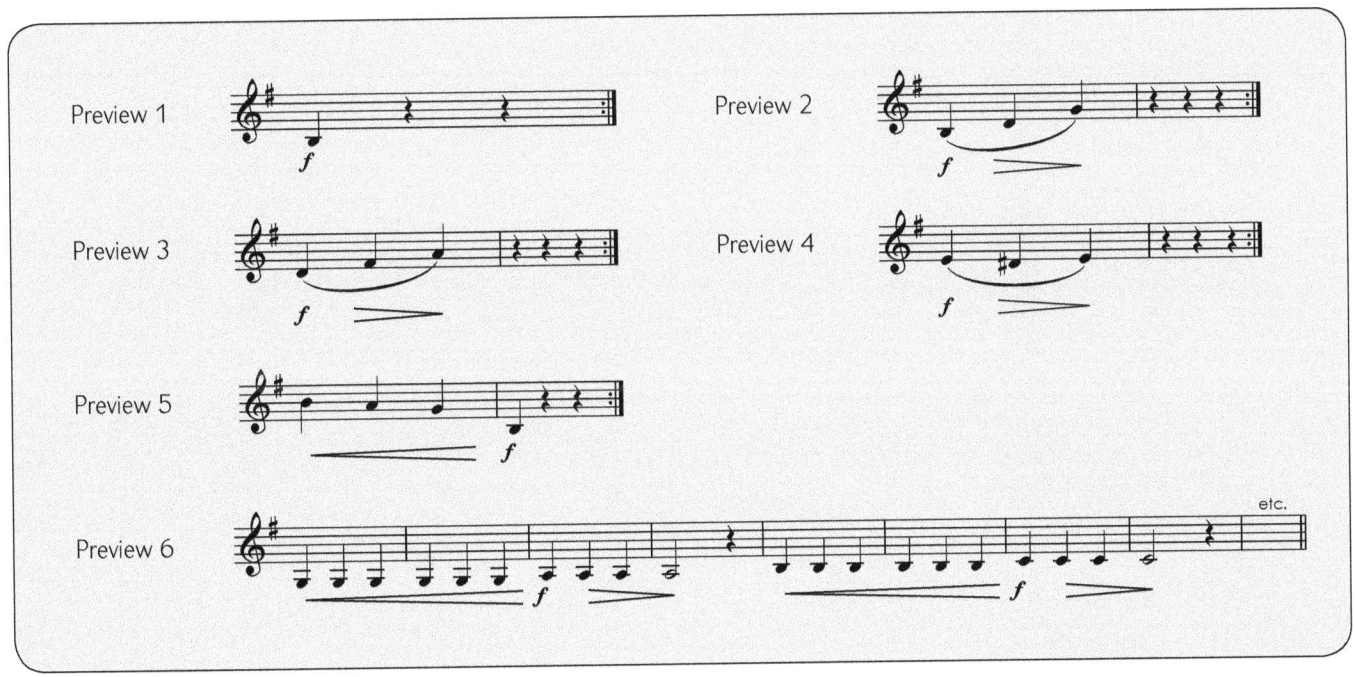

Preview 1

Preview 2

Preview 3

Preview 4

Preview 5

Preview 6

Larry O'Gaff

Irish

D Major

♪ = 126–200,
then ♩. = 66–106

See bowing
pattern p.5

*The humorous ballads "Making Babies by Steam" and "Humors of Whiskey,"
as well as the serious ballad "Cumberland's Crew," also use this tune.*

Grace note
previews

All the Pretty Little Horses

African American

Hush-a-bye, don't you cry / Go to sleepy little ba-by;
When you wake, you shall have / All the pretty little horses.
Dapples and greys, pintos and bays, / Go to sleepy little baby.
Hush-a-bye, don't you cry / Go to sleepy little ba-by.

La saison est bèlle

La SAY-zoh eh BELL-ah
French

See bowing pattern p.5

e minor

♩ = 65–100

Y voi-là ben six mois qu'la saison il est bèlle;
Y voi-là ben six mois qu'la saison il est bèlle;
On voit tous ces amants qui changent de maitrèsses
Le bon vin m'y en-dort, et l'amour m'y réveil-le.

In the springtime, blooming violets on the meadow,
In the summer, purple clover ev'rywhere.
So do lovers with the seasons change their partners
But keep your love close, now that winter's in the air.

Meter change preview

Placing the grace note before the beat

Adding the full rhythm

Anchoring the underlying rhythm and meter

The "Hop-Plop" Bowstroke
Preparation for Sarabande

① Place the bow at the middle. Play a very small up-bow note on open A, stopping the note on the string. Then lift the bow vertically upward, at a right angle to the string. Do this a few times.

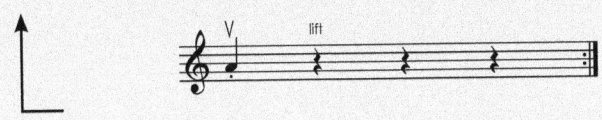

② Now, add an additional step. From the lifted position, return the bow to the string, landing near the frog. The steps are now:

    1. Staccato up-bow "A", pausing on the string.
    2. Vertical lift, followed by a pause.
    3. Return to the string, landing at the frog.

Practice this sequence a few times before moving onto the next step.

③ Now do this three-step sequence, but remove the *first* pause.

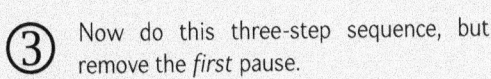

In other words, the transition from horizontal to vertical will now be smooth and continuous. You'll be tracing a curved (rather than square) corner.

Add a moderately long bow back to the starting point (i.e. the **middle** of the bow). The entire sequence uses only the second quarter of the bow.

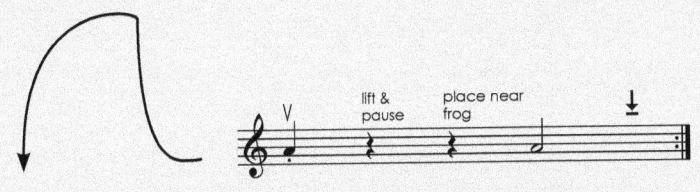

④ Now remove the second pause as well, so all three motions are continuous. Make sure that the peak remains very high — reaching approximately at the level of your eyes.

Put the entire sequence into a four-beat pattern, where beat two consists of a landing followed by a pause. This is the "plop"!

The half note ("half-bow") ends with the bow anchored on the string, ready to begin the next pattern.

Play this four-beat pattern on a scale.

Sarabande

from First Suite for Two Musettes

Joseph Bodin de Boismortier
1689-1755

The ⌐ marking is used throughout this book to indicate a bow lift which starts from the string.

In Sarabande (above) and in Cato's Advice (p.51), each lift is followed by on-the-string playing. In Branle, Kolomyika, Birch Tree, and Bohemian Dance, these lifts are followed by a "strike" (single spiccato note) or several spiccato notes.

These articulations are editorial suggestions only — they are not indicated by the composer. The performer is free to select the articulation and bowstroke which best suit their desired interpretation and technique.

Boots of Shining Leather

Hungarian

e minor

l t d r m l m

If you'd dance then you must have boots of shining leather,
Money in your pocketbook, in your cap a feather.

But if you would sing with me,
You don't need a cent, you see,
So come and sing together!

If you'd dance then you must have boots of shining leather.
If you'd dance then you must have boots of shining leather.

Dimensions of Spiccato

The essential variables of spiccato are:

- Angle of approach (steep or shallow);
- Duration (time) on the string; and
- Weight upon impact (which affects string displacement)

We can talk about the angle and duration variables using the shapes to the right.

What does each of these sound like? Which sound do you want to get on a given passage?

Saucer

Dinner Plate

Soup Bowl

Cereal Bowl

Guided Discovery: The Order of Sharps

Each key that you've played has a consistent set of notes, which sometimes include a mix of natural and sharp notes. Let's find out the names of the notes that belong with each key!

Play a C Major scale on the piano. Are there any black keys in this key?

Now walk up on the following notes: "do, re, mi, fi, so." "Fi" is a raised fourth scale degree. The note you just arrived at, which is G, will become your next *do*.

Play a G Major scale on the piano. Are there any black keys in this key? If so, what are their names?

Now walk up again on "do, re, mi, fi, so." The note you just arrived at, which is D, will become your next *do*.

Play a D Major scale on the piano. Are there any black keys in this key? If so, what are their names?

Do the same process one more time. You will arrive at A.

Play an A Major scale on the piano. Are there any black keys in this key? If so, what are their names?

Notating the Sharp Key Signatures

The sharps go in order by key: F C G D A E B. We can use the mnemonic, "Fancy Cats Go Dancing And Eat Bagels."

If there is one sharp, it is always F♯. If there are two sharps, they are always F♯ and C♯. Three sharps will are always be F♯, C♯, and G♯, and so on.

You can use the last sharp of any key signature to find what key you're in, because it is always "ti."

Instead of writing sharps on every single, notes, we can use a *key signature*. We'll simply take the "usual" sharps or flats that go with a particular key and place them *at the beginning of each staff* ... instead of writing them on the notes. This is useful because:

* It saves the composer from having to write the same sharps (or flats) over and over again.
* It allows the musician playing the piece to see any notes that are "out of the ordinary." These are called *accidentals*.

The *key signature* is written right after the treble clef sign. The sharps are always written in the same places, and they apply to every octave, even though they're only written in one place:

Copy the key signatures below. Write the name of the key after each example.

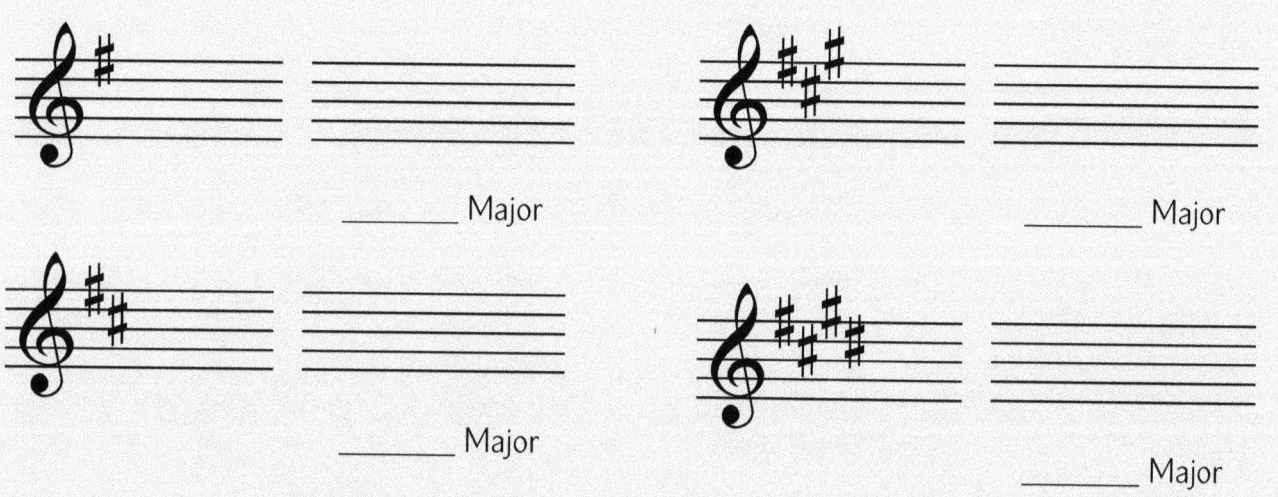

_____ Major

_____ Major

_____ Major

_____ Major

Cato's Advice

Interpone tuis interdum gaudia curis,
ut possis animo quemuis suffere laborem.

Mingle pleasures with your cares, that you may
in good spirit sustain your labors.

Henry Carey
1687–1743

What Ca_to_ advises, most certainly wise_ is
not al_ways to_ labor but sometimes to play;
To min_gle sweet pleasure with search after treasure,
indulging at night for_ the_ toils of the day.

And while the dull miser esteems himself wi_ser,
his bags to increase he_ his_ health will decay.
Our souls we enlighten, our fancies we brigh_ten,
and passing long evenings_ in_ pleasure away.

E Major Review (if needed):

☐ Row, Row   ☐ Under the Spreading Chestnut   ☐ Lavender's Blue   ☐ Piper's Tune   ☐ Petit Oiseau

---

A Bit of History ...

The inscription for this piece (i.e. the quote beneath the title) is from the *The Distichs of Cato*, a collection of wisdom by Dionysius Cato, dating from the 4th century A.D.

"Cato" was the nickname of a schoolbook for teaching Latin, popularly regarded not only as a textbook but as a moral compass. It was among the best-known books from the Middle Ages, and its use continued well into the 18th century. Benjamin Franklin studied Cato, and Geoffrey Chaucer referred to the text in *The Canterbury Tales*.

C Major / A Minor Transposition

C Major is preparation for Golden Slumbers and Branle. A Minor is preparation for Glädjens Blomster.

C Major		a minor	
	SCALE (middle octave)		SCALE
	All My Little Ducklings		All My Little Ducklings
	Twinkle, Twinkle		Twinkle, Twinkle
	Frere Jacques		Frere Jacques
	Yankee Doodle		Petit Oiseau

Golden Slumbers

English

C Major

Golden slumbers kiss your eyes,
Smiles awake you when you rise,
Sleep, pretty lov_'d ones, do_ not cry_
And I will sing a lullaby.
Lullaby, Lullaby, Lu_llaby.

The author's source for this song was the *Golden Book of Favorite Songs* (Minneapolis, 1941) which credits the song as a 17th Century lullaby. Further research reveals that the lyrics were written by Thomas Dekker (1572-1632) as a poem in the play *Patient Grissel*, published in 1603. Much later, the Beatles adapted these lyrics to their own version of a song, with an original melody by Paul McCartney, in their album *Abbey Road*, released in 1969.

Birch Tree

Russian

Anchored lift followed
by spiccato, with string
crossing

Branle de l'official

BRAHN duh loh-fee-SHUHL
French, circa 1500

 See bowing pattern p.11

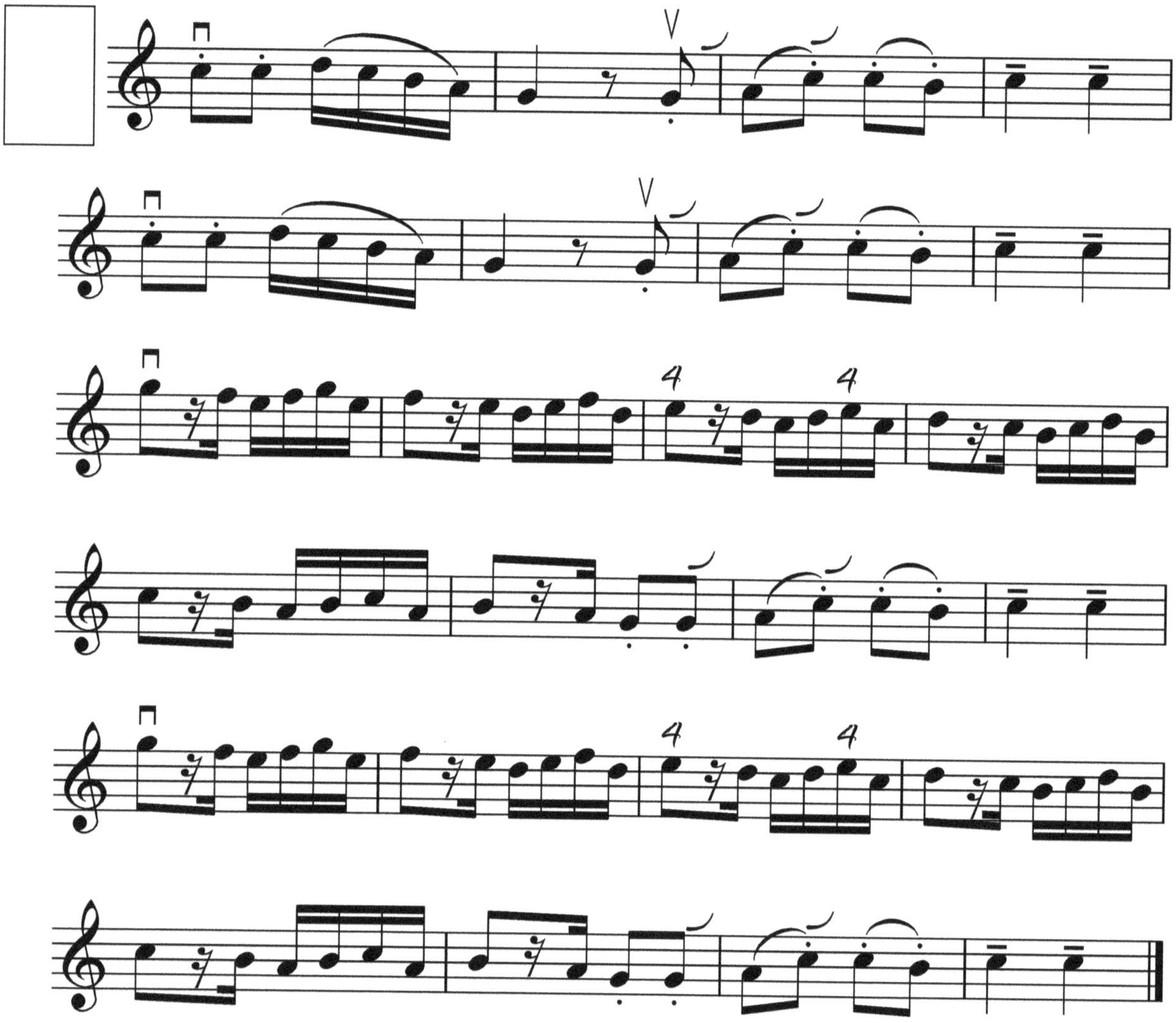

Tuning Exercise:
Diagonal First Finger

Pattern Extraction
(for speed work)

Kolomyika

Koh-LOH-myee-ka
Ukrainian

spiccato

Fine

D.C. al Fine

Third Finger Chromatic
Leading Tone Preview

Place both
fingers together

See bowing
pattern p.5

G Major

B♭ Major / G Minor Transposition

Preparation for Glädjens Blomster

B♭ Major		g minor	
	SCALE		SCALE
	Twinkle, Twinkle		Twinkle, Twinkle
	Frere Jacques		Frere Jacques
	Yankee Doodle		Petit oiseau
	Row, Row		All the Pretty Little Horses
	Momiji		
	Galway Piper		
	Nu ska vi skörda linet		

Second Position Transposition (F Major)

Preparation for Vibrato Practice. *Applying a temporary first finger tape is suggested.*

	F Major scale		Frere Jacques
	All My Little Ducklings		This Old Man
	Mary Had a Little Lamb		Toddy-O
	Twinkle, Twinkle		Under the Spreading Chestnut

Glädjens blomster

GLEDD-yens BLOHM-stuh
Swedish, "Flowers of Gladness"

Glädjens blomster i jordens mull, ack, visst aldrig gro.
Kärlek själv ju försåtlig är för ditt hjärtas ro.
Men där ovan, för hopp och tro, blomstra de evigt friska.
Hör du ej hur andar ljuvt om dem till hjärtat viska?

Flow'rs of joy from the mould'ring earth, surely ne'er can grow
And the love that may touch your heart soon may turn to woe.
There above, hope and faith abide, flow'rs fragrant bloom forever
In the night I hear the flowers to my spirit whisper.

English translation by Elise Winters © 2017

Bohemian Dance

Czech

 See bowing
pattern p.5

D Major

For the strongest sound and best bow control, Bohemian Dance
should be played entirely in the lower ⅓ of the bow.

Reference

Training the *Vibrato*

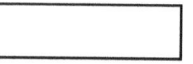

Vibrato Study Assignment

Watch videos of a few soloists playing the pieces below. Write the name of each soloist to the right. Place a ✱ next to whose vibrato you would most like to emulate.

• Tchaikovsky Canzonetta • Meditation from Thais • Wieniawski Romance •

_____

_____

_____

Teeter Totter *Learning to selectively turn "off" the muscles of the left arm.*

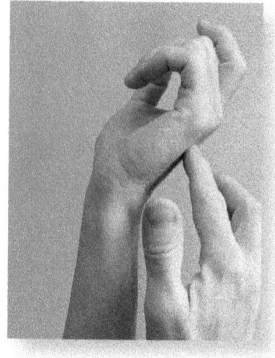
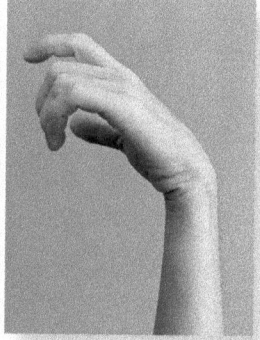

1. Place the left (violin) arm in playing position, with the arm vertical. Allow the hand to fall backward.

2. With the index of your bow hand, give the violin hand a quick nudge, enough to tip it to the other side, like tipping a see saw. The practice parent can also do this.

3. Repeat these steps until the left arm can remain passive and relaxed.

4. When ready, wobble the hand to and fro, making sure the motion is loose and free. The nudges are now coming from a teeny, tiny "throwing" motion in the arm. You are using your hand like a pendulum!

Shaker Egg *Keeping the wrist loose, while using the flexors to hold a lightweight object.*

Fill a pill bottle or plastic egg with a small amount of rice, salt, or dried beans. Repeat the above movement, cradling the egg loosely in the curve of the fingers.

TIP: Don't focus on the shaking sound. Instead focus on a relaxed "seesaw" motion, using a tiny movement of your arm to "bounce" your hand from side to side.

Practice this exercise to a steady beat, starting around ♩ =50. Use the vibrato backing tracks on page 64 to gradually increase your tempo.

Once you achieve a relaxed, consistent oscillation at ♩ =90, you can move on to the next exercise.

Heads Up!!! You'll Be a Guitarist for a Few Months.

Most of the steps for vibrato will be learned in rest position. This enables you to see how all of the relevant parts are moving, and frees you from supporting the violin during these stages.

For each of the steps below, you will first establish the correct angle and direction of motion.

Then you will work to increase your speed, using a metronome as well as the backing tracks provided at the end of the section.

Once you develop muscle memory for the motions in rest position, transferring everything into playing position will be surprisingly easy. You'll be vibrating in no time!

Thumb Swings *Pivoting the hand while the thumb is fastened in place.*

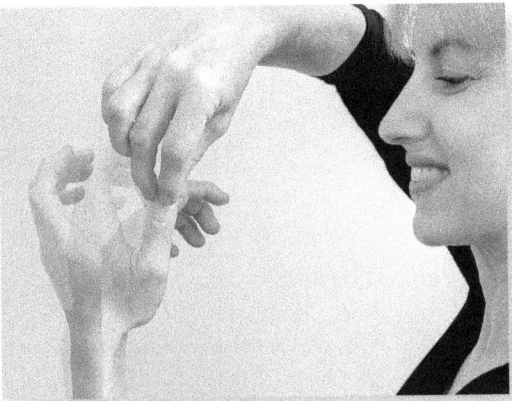

- Be sure the hand, not the thumb, is aligned with the arm. The thumb should be left of center. Don't pull the thumb out, down or forward.
- Make sure not to *rotate* around the axis of the thumb. Instead, imagine you're throwing the palm of your hand. The pinky side is just along for the ride.
- The fingers are passengers and should stay "asleep." Make sure they don't extend, flap, or wiggle. Keep them relaxed, curved, and slightly lifted.
- The hand should pivot equally on both sides, like a seesaw. Even with the thumb "pinned," the motion should feel almost as loose as before.

PREQUEL: Gently place the tip of your left thumb between your front teeth. Rock the hand forward and back. This is an easy way to experience the motion you're about to practice.

PALM DOWN: Face your palm toward the floor. Fasten the tip of your thumb with your right hand, and hold it stationary while you bounce an imaginary ball with your left hand.

VIOLIN POSITION: Rotate your arm into vertical position, with the palm facing right. It's fine to do this in front of the body. Hold your thumb by reaching overtop or by pinching both sides from the front. The practice partner can also hold the thumb.

Pivot the palm forward and back in a rolling (rather than staccato) motion.

Practice Thumb Swings to a steady beat, starting around ♩=70. Use the vibrato backing tracks on page 64 to gradually increase your tempo. Once you achieve a relaxed, consistent oscillation at ♩=100, you can move on to the next exercise.

Neck Polishes

Establishing the direction of vibrato along the neck of the violin.

Do this exercise in rest position.

Mark the knuckle of the first finger with an "x." With the violin in rest position, touch the knuckle to the violin neck. Use a whole-arm motion to glide forward and back (toward and away from the scroll), keeping the knuckle touching (sliding on the "x") the whole time.

Next, add the thumb, so that you are gliding with two points of contact.

The fingers should float in the air, gently curved.

If perspiration prevents your hand or thumb from moving freely, dust your hand with a bit of cornstarch.

Thumb Swings on the Violin *Transferring the Thumb Swing motion to the violin neck.*

Do this exercise in rest position.

Again in rest position, place the hand in second position. This gives you room on both sides.

Do neck polishes, but this time keep your thumb fastened, pivoting from the wrist. The moving part is the palm of the hand. The fingers should stay "asleep."

A slight bit of hanging pressure on the thumb should be sufficient to maintain it in place.

Make sure the knuckle of your pointer finger brushes the neck at all times. This helps ensure that your hand is moving forward and back rather than rotating or "flipping."

Teacher Note: It is best to demonstrate this exercise and Sandcastles & Puddles in a segmented fashion, pausing between each position. A fluid oscillation is often too fast for students to reproduce correctly.

Once the correct motion has been trained in discrete segments, it can be put into a fluid oscillation.

Practice Thumb Swings daily for 5–10 minutes, starting around ♩ = 60. Use the vibrato backing tracks on page 64 to gradually increase your tempo. Once you achieve a relaxed, consistent oscillation at ♩ =110, you can move on to the next exercise.

Water Slide & Zipline

Do this exercise in rest position.

Adding a finger touch to the Thumb Swing motion.

WATER SLIDE: With the violin in rest position, place your hand in second position. Rest the tip of the *middle finger* lightly between the A and E strings. Your fingernail should approximately face the bridge.

Move your hand forward and back, sliding in the groove between the strings.

- The finger should maintain its square shape; it should not extend or lengthen. The finger should not hop or jump.
- Focus on moving the *back* of the hand. The finger is just a passenger.

ZIPLINE: Do the same motion, but sliding along the A or E string.

Practice Water Slide or Zipline daily for 5–10 minutes. Begin at your current comfortable tempo and use the backing tracks to gradually increase your speed. The goal is a relaxed, consistent oscillation at ♩ =120.

Doorbell Fingers

Training the finger to be soft enough to flex, but firm enough to remain anchored on the fingerboard.

Make a circle with your middle finger and thumb, using a medium pressure. Use the right hand to gently push (and then release) the first knuckle. It should bounce back. *Also experiment with a pressure that is too firm (it won't bounce back) or too loose (it will fall off).*

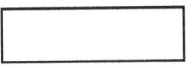 ## Sandcastles & Puddles: Arm Motion

Establishing the flexibility of the finger joints while anchoring the fingertip.

1. With your violin in rest position and your hand in second position, place your *first finger* on the E or A string. Anchor your fingertip gently into the fingerboard. The thumb should be in a gentle inward curve. *Make sure your entire arm is perfectly straight, including the wrist.*

2. Move your *entire arm* back toward the scroll, keeping the fingertip anchored. Your arm will pull down the finger, causing it to flatten.

3. Return to the original position. *Make sure the finger returns to a square shape. The index finger knuckle should touch the violin neck throughout. Be sure that your pinky doesn't curl into the palm of your hand.*

4. Repeat these steps, pausing each time to check your finger square.

5. Practice the motion on second finger.

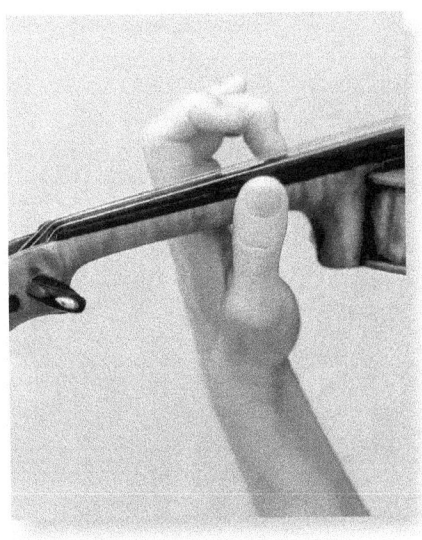

Sandcastles & Puddles: Wrist Motion

As above, but with the additional challenge of pivoting from the wrist.

Do the Sandcastles and Puddles motion using a hand tilt (i.e. pivoting from the wrist) rather than a full-arm motion. The hand, not the finger, should drive the motion.

Optionally, use your right arm (reaching under the violin) to grasp the left forearm and hold it in place, to more easily isolate the wrist motion.

Practice "Sandcastles & Puddles" for 5–10 minutes a day. Start with single movements, checking your finger angle at each step. Take your time, being very accurate in each movement.

Next, begin building your speed, from ♩ = 46 (the slowest speed on the backing tracks) to ♩ = 130 with two motions per beat.

You're doing vibrato! You'll put it on your shoulder in the next step.

Do this exercise in rest position.

Sandcastles & Puddles with arm motion

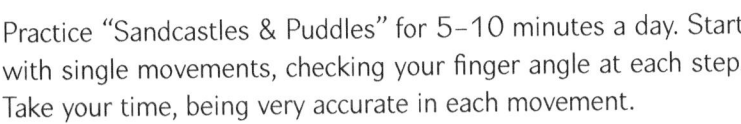 ## Use the Fingertip to Anchor Your Hand

One of the paradoxes of vibrato is that activating the finger flexors (i.e. pressing the string) causes our bodies to instinctively firm up the wrist joint; BUT having that fingertip well-anchored is what provides the security to oscillate your hand most freely and with sufficient amplitude.

How do we resolve this paradox?

1) Think of *leaning* into your finger. You're looking for the geometry for transferring weight using angle more than strength. The "lean" will feel different as the finger shape (i.e. geometry) changes.

2) Learn to decouple the firmness of your finger with the looseness of your wrist. (That's one of the main goals of these exercises!)

Even as the angle changes, continue leaning into your finger — just as you might lean onto your elbow at different angles.

Pop Song "Backing Tracks" for Vibrato Practice

Practicing your vibrato exercises along with music makes it more enjoyable! It also offers the following benefits:

- Vibrato practice benefits from a certain looseness of attention. You want to be focused enough to make sure the motion is correct, but relaxed enough for your body to discover your hand's natural oscillation. The music will help you to find this "fuzzy" mental space, with your mind balancing fluidly between the music and the movement.

- Having a musical accompaniment will allow you to find a fluid, legato motion, whereas practicing directly with the metronome will tend to encourage a more staccato motion.

- The music will also allow you to practice longer, allowing you to reach your vibrato dreams much sooner!

Start at the slowest speed, making sure your movement is correct. Every so often, throw in a few motions in double time, then return to your original speed.

Move through the songs, gradually increasing your speed.

2 MOVEMENTS / BEAT	♩ =
Lifandi vatnið (Living Water) *Ásgeir Trausti*	46
Saman *Ólafur Arnalds*	65
Gnossienne no.1 *Erik Satie, pianist Alexandre Tharaud*	54
Dearly Beloved (Kindom Hearts II version) *Yoko Shimomura*	58
Gone Angels *Mili*	65
Green Onions *Booker T. & the M.G.'s*	65
Elements *Lindsey Stirling*	72
A Million Dreams *The Greatest Showman*	75
What Was I Made For? *Billie Eilish*	80
Happy (Despicable Me) *Pharrell Williams*	80
Koya Blues *Abou Diarra*	80
Bittersweet Symphony *The Verve*	86
Bad Moon Rising *Creedence Clearwater Revival*	91
Nuala's Tune *Maura Shawn Scanlin*	91
Hiya, Hiya *Eljoee*	96
On Top of the World *Imagine Dragons*	101
We Don't Talk About Bruno *Encanto*	104
Loup Andalou *Mathias Duplessy*	106
Sonkolon *Fatoumata Diawara*	106
The Osprey *Dougie MacLean*	109
Don't Stop Believin' *Journey*	119
Red Rocket *The Fitzgeralds*	120
Fiddler's Despair *Natalie McMaster*	127

	♩ =
Let's Get Loud *Jennifer Lopez*	134
Born to Be Wild *Steppenwolf*	149
Caribbean Blue *Enya*	152
4 MOVEMENTS / BEAT	
Un air de liberté *Khaled Mouzanar*	57
Viva La Vida *Coldplay*	70
Monte *Rumba Tumba*	74
La Bamba *Los Lobos*	79
Cuatro Vientos *Danit*	81
The Arena *Lindsey Stirling*	89
Tarha Tadagh *Imarhan*	94
Mountains O' Things *Tracy Chapman*	94
Mindjer dôce mel *Eneida Marta*	94
White Rabbit *Jefferson Airplane*	104
Try Everything *Shakira (Zootopia)*	115

A Spotify playlist of these songs can be found here:

discoverviolin.org/vibrato

| | Rockin' Rhythms

Increasing the control, fluency, versatility, and automaticity of the vibrato.

Practice vibrating each finger in different rhythms, to a different finger either on every pattern or every phrase of the song. The songs may be practiced along with the recording. This may be done either in rest position or playing position (once introduced).

- ❐ Rapid single pulses ("ribbets")
- ❐ Double ribbets (two quick pulses in a row)
- ❐ Peanut Butter Cracker
- ❐ Paw Paw Patch

- ❐ Galway Piper
- ❐ Polly Wolly Doodle
- ❐ Shortnin' Bread
- ❐ Kolomyika

| | Wobbles in Playing Position

Transferring the vibrato motion to shoulder position.

With your violin on your shoulder, place the thumb slightly under the neck of the violin, and the second finger in second position on the A string. The elbow should be at D string angle (i.e. slightly forward).

Use your right hand to stabilize the body of the violin. This will free your left hand from the need to support the instrument.

1. Warm up with Water Slide & Zipline in playing position. *A slight gap between your hand and the neck of the violin is okay — about the width of a credit card.*

2. Do Sandcastles & Puddles (with wrist movement) in playing position.

3. When you're ready, do 10 counts of wobbles, then bow two long notes. Continue alternating with and without the bow.

If your vibrato motion starts to get disorganized, go back to rest position. Silent practice in playing position is also helpful.

If you want to have a beautiful vibrato in six months, strive for a "wobbly" sounding vibrato right now. That means it's wide enough! Your vibrato will continue developing over the next couple years. As it gets faster, keep it wide and loose.

Use the backing tracks to begin building your speed. Start with your current comfortable speed and work up to ♩ = 152 with two motions per beat, making sure the motion remains loose.

Once this is accomplished, continue increasing to the final goal of ♩ = 115 with FOUR motions per beat.

Some important reminders during this final step:

- Watch your pinky! If it is curled into the palm of your hand, your arm will be too tense to oscillate freely.
- Make sure your thumb remains in a curved, "banana" shape, supporting the violin from underneath the neck.

2-3-2-1-2 in Second Position

Moving the vibrato from one finger to the next.

This exercise uses the ease of the second finger to help train all the other fingers.
Playing with the harmony can help to focus the intonation during this stage.

Teacher Harmony (optional)

Songs with Vibrato

In reality any song may be played with vibrato as long as it is slowed down enough. However, this list offers a starting point
Start by vibrating the longest notes, then gradually add the surrounding notes.

- ☐ Twinkle, Twinkle (2nd position)
- ☐ Arroró (2nd position)
- ☐ Poor Little Kitty (2nd position)
- ☐ Row, Row Your Boat
- ☐ Pretty Little Horses

- ☐ Dobrú Noc
- ☐ Momiji
- ☐ Golden Slumbers
- ☐ Under the Spreading Chestnut Tree
- ☐ Glädjens blomster

My Weekly Listening

Date	Piece	Composer	Artist

Assignments & Completion Record

My current
vibrato step: _____

Focus on: _____

My current
tempo: _____

Minutes
per day: _____

☆	♩	🎹 🎼		
			Under the Spreading Chestnut page 13	
			Hollahi, Hollaho 14	
			Les petites marionnettes 15	
			Marionnettes: Piano Countermelody 16	
			Kookaburra 17	
			Lavender's Blue 19	
			Weekly Listening 67	
			Piper's Tune 21	
			Lavender's Blue: Rhythm & Beat 22	
			Row, Row, Row Your Boat 23	
			Beat Discovery of Row, Row 23	
			Bluebells of Scotland 25	
			Polly Wolly Doodle 26	
			Petit oiseau 27	
			Har du sett min far 28	
			Giroflé, girofla 29	
			Nu ska vi skörda linet idag 31	
			What Can the Matter Be 34	
			E Minor Transposition 40	

TEACHER NOTE: The second column provides a place to mark the successful completion of the song notation. The third column can be used to assign and graduate the student's playing the song with the metronome, or with the piano recording. For assignments with only one column, it simply indicates successful completion.

Plan Your Book 2 Graduation Recital

Day, date, and time: _____

Location: _____

Who will attend? (at least four guests besides immediate family)

_____ _____

_____ _____

_____ _____

_____

Where will you hold the after-concert reception? _____

What re-arranging or decor will be needed for the concert and/or reception? _____

REPERTOIRE SELECTION:

Two fast, lively songs (one with spiccato): _____

Two slow songs: _____

Baroque or Renaissance song*: _____

Fun, relaxed song: _____

Two more songs (your choice): _____

*Songs which meet this criterion are Sarabande, Branle, and Cato's Advice.

What accompaniment would you like to use?

____ Live pianist   ____ Violin duet   ____ None

____ Piano recording   ____ Combination

Make sure to have at least THREE "practice" recitals during the two weeks before your recital.
One of these should be in whatever shoes and outfit you plan to wear.

Have fun, and enjoy your special day!